iPod
The Missing Manual

Seventh Edition

iPod: The Missing Manual, Seventh Edition

BY J.D. BIERSDORFER WITH DAVID POGUE

Copyright © 2009 J. D. Biersdorfer. All rights reserved.
Printed in Canada.

Published by O'Reilly Media, Inc., 1005 Gravenstein Highway North, Sebastopol, CA 95472.

O'Reilly books may be purchased for educational, business, or sales promotional use. Online editions are also available for most titles (*safari.oreilly.com*). For more information, contact our corporate/institutional sales department: 800.998.9938 or corporate@*oreilly.com*.

Executive Editor: Laurie Petrycki

Editor: Peter Meyers

Production Editor: Nellie McKesson

Illustrations: Rob Romano and Lesley Keegan

Indexer: Julie Hawks

Cover Designers: Randy Comer, Karen Montgomery, and Suzy Wiviott

Interior Designer: Ron Bilodeau

Print History:

October 2008: First Edition.

ISBN-13: 978-0-596-52212-4

[F]

Contents

Chapter 5

Chapter 6

Chapter 7

The Missing Credits

About the Authors

J.D. Biersdorfer is co-author of both *The Internet: The Missing Manual* and the second edition of *Google: The Missing Manual*. She's been writing the weekly computer Q&A column for *The New York Times* since 1998 and has covered everything from 17th-century Indian art to the world of female hackers for the newspaper. She's also written articles for the *AIGA Journal of Graphic Design* and *Rolling Stone* and has contributed essays about the collision of art and technology to several graphic-design books published by Allworth Press. She studied in the Theater & Drama program at Indiana University and now spends her limited spare moments playing the banjo and watching BBC World News. Email: jd.biersdorfer@gmail.com.

David Pogue (co-author) is the weekly tech columnist for the *New York Times*, an Emmy-winning correspondent for *CBS News Sunday Morning*, weekly CNBC contributor, and the creator of the Missing Manual series. He's the author or co-author of 47 books, including 22 in this series and six in the *"For Dummies"* line (including *Macs, Magic, Opera*, and *Classical Music*). In his other life, David is a former Broadway show conductor, a piano player, and a magician.

Links to his columns and weekly videos await at *www.davidpogue.com*. He welcomes feedback about his books by email at *david@pogueman.com*.

About the Creative Team

Peter Meyers (editor) is the managing editor of the Missing Manual series. He lives with his wife, daughter, and cats in New York City. Email: *meyers@oreilly.com*.

Nellie McKesson (production editor) lives in Jamaica Plain, Mass., where she makes t-shirts for her friends (*mattsaundersbynellie.etsy.com*) and plays music with her band Dr. & Mrs. Van Der Trampp. Email: *nellie@oreilly.com*.

Acknowledgements

I would like to thank David Pogue for suggesting this book to me way back in 2002, and then being a terrific editor through the mad scramble of the first two editions—and for providing his cheerful expertise for this edition. Also thanks to editor Peter Meyers for guiding me through the past five updates. Thanks to Ron Bilodeau, Lesley Keegan, Chris Stone, and the Missing Manual folks at O'Reilly, and to Apple for courteously providing the iPod images and the assorted other iPod accessory companies who made their digital photography available. I'd also to thank all my friends and family (especially and most importantly, Betsy) for putting up with me that time every year when Apple announces new iPods and I disappear into my computer for several weeks, muttering incoherently and cranking up Steve Earle to a hearty volume level.

The Missing Manual Series

Missing Manuals are witty, superbly written guides to computer products that don't come with printed manuals (which is just about all of them). Each book features a handcrafted index and RepKover, a detached-spine binding that lets the book lie perfectly flat without the assistance of weights or cinder blocks.

Recent and upcoming titles include:

Access 2007: The Missing Manual by Matthew MacDonald

AppleScript: The Missing Manual by Adam Goldstein

Creating Web Sites: The Missing Manual by Matthew MacDonald

CSS: The Missing Manual by David Sawyer McFarland

David Pogue's Digital Photography: The Missing Manual by David Pogue

Dreamweaver CS4: The Missing Manual by David Sawyer McFarland

Excel 2003: The Missing Manual by Matthew MacDonald

Excel 2007: The Missing Manual by Matthew MacDonald

FileMaker Pro 9: The Missing Manual by Geoff Coffey and Susan Prosser

Flash CS4: The Missing Manual by Chris Grover

FrontPage 2003: The Missing Manual by Jessica Mantaro

Google: The Missing Manual, Second Edition by Sarah Milstein, J.D. Biersdorfer, and Matthew MacDonald

Google Apps: The Missing Manual by Nancy Conner

iMovie '08: The Missing Manual by David Pogue

iPhoto '08: The Missing Manual by David Pogue

iPhone: The Missing Manual, Second Edition by David Pogue

JavaScript: The Missing Manual by David Sawyer McFarland

Mac OS X Leopard: The Missing Manual, by David Pogue

Office 2004 for Macintosh: The Missing Manual by Mark H. Walker and Franklin Tessler

Office 2008 for Macintosh: The Missing Manual by Jim Elferdink

Photoshop CS4: The Missing Manual by Lesa Snider King

Photoshop Elements 6 for Mac: The Missing Manual by Barbara Brundage

Photoshop Elements 7: The Missing Manual by Barbara Brundage

PowerPoint 2007: The Missing Manual by Emily Moore

QuickBooks 2009: The Missing Manual by Bonnie Biafore

Quicken 2009: The Missing Manual by Bonnie Biafore

Switching to the Mac: The Missing Manual, Leopard Edition by David Pogue

The Internet: The Missing Manual by David Pogue and J.D. Biersdorfer

Wikipedia: The Missing Manual by John Broughton

Windows XP Home Edition: The Missing Manual, Second Edition by David Pogue

Windows Vista: The Missing Manual by David Pogue

Windows Vista for Starters: The Missing Manual by David Pogue

Word 2007: The Missing Manual by Chris Grover

Your Brain: The Missing Manual by Matthew MacDonald

Introduction

Like the arrival of the Sony Walkman, which revolutionized the personal listening experience, Apple's introduction of the iPod in the fall of 2001 caught the world's ear. "With iPod, listening to music will never be the same again," intoned Steve Jobs, Apple's CEO. But even outside the Hyperbolic Chamber, the iPod was different enough to get attention. People noticed it, and more importantly, bought it.

If you're reading this book, odds are you're one of these folks. Or maybe you've just upgraded to a new iPod—Classic, Nano, Shuffle, or Touch—and want to learn about all the new features. In any case, welcome aboard!

With today's iPods, you can watch Hollywood feature films and TV shows, play popular video games, display gorgeous full-color photos, and look up personal phone numbers. If you have an iPod Touch, you can also surf the Web, buy music wirelessly, and spend hours exploring the wonders of YouTube with no bulky computer necessary. You can quickly find out how to do all of that within these pages—and also learn everything you need to know about iTunes, the iPod's desktop software companion.

Three iPods can play video now: the latest Nanos, the Classic, and especially the smooth, sleek iPod Touch in all its widescreen glory. And all models still crank out the music—including the tiny clip-on iPod Shuffle, the loudest lapel pin on the market. But no matter which iPod you have, it's time to load it up with the music and other stuff that's important to you. Even the smallest model can hold hundreds of songs and play the Soundtrack of Your Life in any order you'd like.

Steve Jobs was right about the iPod. Things just haven't been the same since.

How to Use This Book

The tiny pamphlet that Apple includes in each iPod package is enough to get your iPod up and running, charged, and ready to download music.

But if you want to know more about how the iPod works, all the great things it can do, and where to find its secret features, the official pamphlet is skimpy in the extreme. And the iTunes help files that you have to read on your computer screen aren't much better: You can't mark your place or underline anything, there aren't any pictures or jokes, and you can't read them in the bathroom without fear of electrocution. This book lets you do all that, gives you more iPod info than the wee brochure, *and* it has nice color pictures.

About→These→Arrows

Throughout this book, and throughout the Missing Manual series, you'll find sentences like this one: "Open the View→Show Equalizer" menu. That's short-hand for a longer series of instructions that go something like: "Go to the menu bar in iTunes, click the View menu, and then select the Show Equalizer entry." Our shorthand system helps keep things much more snappy than those long, drawn out instructions.

The Very Basics

To use this book, and indeed to use a computer, you need to know a few basics. This book assumes that you're familiar with a few terms and concepts:

- **Clicking.** To *click* means to point the arrow cursor at something on the screen and then to press and release the clicker button on the mouse (or laptop trackpad). To *double-click*, of course, means to click twice in rapid succession, again without moving the cursor at all. To *drag* means to move the cursor *while* pressing the button.

When you're told to *Ctrl+click* something on a PC, or ⌘-*click* something on the Mac, you click while pressing the Ctrl or ⌘ key (both of which are near the Space bar).

- **Menus.** The *menus* are the words at the top of your screen or window: File, Edit, and so on. Click one to make a list of commands appear, as though they're written on a window shade you've just pulled down.

- **Keyboard shortcuts.** Jumping up to menus in iTunes *takes* time. Many keyboard quickies that perform the same menu functions are sprinkled throughout the book—Windows shortcuts first, followed by Mac shortcuts in parentheses, just like this: "To quickly summon the Preferences box press Ctrl+comma (⌘-comma)."

If you've mastered this much information, you have all the technical background you need to enjoy *iPod: The Missing Manual*.

About MissingManuals.com

At the Web site, click the "Missing CD" link to reveal a neat, organized, chapter-by-chapter list of the shareware and freeware mentioned in this book. The Web site also offers corrections and updates to the book (to see them, click the book's title, then click Errata). In fact, you're invited and encouraged to submit such corrections and updates yourself. In an effort to keep the book as up to date and accurate as possible, each time we print more copies of this book, we'll make any confirmed corrections you've suggested.

We'll also note such changes on the Web site, so that you can mark important corrections in your own copy of the book, if you like. And we'll keep the book current as Apple releases more iPods and software updates. While you're online, you can also register this book at *www.oreilly.com* (you can jump directly to the registration page by going here: *http://tinyurl.com/yo82k3*). Registering means we can send you updates about this book, and you'll be eligible for special offers like discounts on future editions of *iPod: The Missing Manual*.

Safari® Books Online

Safari••⟩
Books Online

When you see a Safari® Books Online icon on the cover of your favorite technology book that means the book is available online through the O'Reilly Network Safari Bookshelf.

Safari offers a solution that's better than e-books. It's a virtual library that lets you easily search thousands of top tech books, cut and paste code samples, download chapters, and find quick answers when you need the most accurate, current information. Try it for free at *http://safari.oreilly.com*.

Meet the iPod: Out of the Box and into Your Ears in 15 Minutes

I f you're like most people, you don't want to waste time getting your spiffy new iPod up and running. You probably don't want to wade through anything longer than a couple of paragraphs. Oh, and you'd like some color pictures, too.

Sure, Apple thoughtfully includes a little pamphlet of starter info with every iPod it sells. It's nicely designed as far as pamphlets go. But you may find that it doesn't go far enough. You want more help than a few line drawings and some haiku-like instructions.

This book—especially this chapter—can help you out.

You won't get bogged down in a bland gray ocean of print here. You'll learn a bit about your particular iPod model and how to get it whistling sweet tunes in your ear in a minimal amount of time. If you want more information on in-depth iPodding or getting the most out of iTunes, you can find that stuff in chapters farther down the road.

But for now, it's time to get rolling with your new iPod. Ready?

Meet the iPod Classic

In just a few short years, Apple has transformed the iPod from a humble little 5-gigabyte music player with a black-and-white screen into a full color, gorgeous portable media system that can play movies, TV shows, and video games—all while still fitting comfortably in the palm of your hand. And it's come a long way from those first 5 gigabytes: now you can stuff 120 gigabytes of music, photos, videos, and more onto it.

In those 120 gigabytes, you can fit 30,000 songs or 150 hours of video. And you don't have to stock up on the Duracells, either, because the iPod's rechargeable battery can play audio for 36 hours or last for 6 hours if you're glued to your video library.

The iPod Classic comes in either silver or black. Unlike earlier iPods that sported hard glossy plastic on the front, Apple's latest version comes outfitted in a full metal jacket—anodized aluminum on the front and shiny stainless steel on the back.

Along with the click wheel—think of it as the iPod's mouse—the 2.5-inch color screen is the player's other main element. Capable of displaying more than 65,000 colors at a resolution of 320 by 240 pixels (translation: high-quality), the iPod's a great place to store and show off your latest vacation photos. In fact, you can have up to 25,000 pictures on your 'Pod. The screen also makes it a delight to catch up on that episode of *The Daily Show* you missed, or play a few rounds of solitaire while listening to your favorite music or podcast.

The iPod comes with everything you need to hook it up to your Windows PC or Macintosh: a USB 2.0 cable. You also get those iconic see-what-I've-got white earphones. Once you get up and iPodding, you'll find that everyone and their grandmother wants to sell you other iPod accessories—all you have to do is stroll down to your favorite computer store and browse the ever increasing selection of cases, cables, battery chargers, and more.

Meet the iPod Shuffle

The smallest member of Team iPod doesn't have a screen—but it doesn't need one, because it's designed for fuss-free music on the go. And you don't have to worry about losing your Shuffle, because it clips right to your lapel or pocket—it's like jewelry you can rock out with. Take your pick of five different Shuffle colors: blue, red, green, pink, and silver. You can get it with a 1-gigabyte memory chip (about 240 songs) or a 2-gigabyte model (500 songs). And just because it's called the iPod Shuffle, doesn't mean you have to shuffle your music; you can play your tracks in order with the nudge of a button (see step 3, below).

This petite 'Pod is so tiny, it doesn't even have room for a USB jack, like the one other iPods use to plug into the computer for music-loading and battery-recharging. The Shuffle, which offers about 12 hours of playing time, includes a tiny dock that connects the player to your computer's USB port. In addition to the dock, you also get:

❶ Those trademark white Apple headphones, all ready to plug into the headphone jack on the top of the Shuffle.

❷ A handy control ring on the front of the player to adjust your volume and skip over songs you're not in the mood to hear.

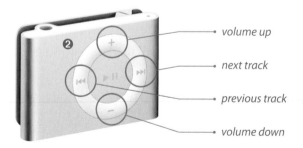

❸ Little silver switches on bottom of the Shuffle to turn it off and on, and to flip between shuffling your songs and playing them in order.

Meet the iPod Nano

The iPod Nano is Apple's mid-sized music player, but it doesn't just look like a regular iPod that got shrunk in the wash. The Nano has its own sleek, stylish design that brings a touch of fashion to your music experience. Like the Classic iPod, the Nano has a color screen and it plays songs, podcasts, and audio books. It can display photos, text notes, contacts, and calendars, too. Unlike Nanos from olden times, today's Nano also *plays video*. You navigate through all these goodies using the smooth, touch-sensitive click wheel.

With its 2-inch color screen and the same sharp 320 by 240-pixel resolution its Classic cousin uses, the Nano can also play movies and many of the same games. But the Nano's even better for workouts because it uses a flash memory chip to store everything. That means it's much more tolerant of jumping and flying around than the Classic Pod, with its big ol' hard drive tucked inside.

The Nano comes in two sizes: 8-gigabyte and 16-gigabyte, all wrapped in scratch-resistant anodized aluminum. You're not just stuck with two colors when buying a Nano, either—you get a rainbow of nine choices: silver, black, purple, blue, green, yellow, orange, red, and pink. Oh, and if you like your music flowing all day long, you'll be glad to know the Nano's battery lasts up to 24 hours—you'll probably conk out before it does.

The Nano has a few other tricks under its aluminum hood. For one thing, it's got a built-in accelerometer (tilt sensor), which means it can sense movement and which way you're holding it. Turn it sideways to watch a movie and see the picture instantly spin around and orient itself for the wider view.

The accelerometer is shaking things up in another way, too—literally. Not in the mood for that song that just came on? Give your Nano a shake to have it shuffle up a new tune. And certain video games were made with the Nano in mind, making you tilt and move your way through the pixelated landscape in search of that next level.

The Nano is also the most accessible iPod ever for visually impaired listeners. An optional Spoken Menus feature recites the names of songs, albums, artists, and menus out loud, letting you navigate through this iPod's content with verbal cues. And for those tired of squinting: The onscreen font size can be made larger, if you like.

At about a quarter of an inch think and tipping the scales at a mere 1.3 ounces, who'd have thought it'd be this easy to fit a combination jukebox/movie theater/handheld gaming console in your pocket?

Meet the iPod Touch

If an iPod Nano and Apple's iPhone ever had a kid, it would surely look something like the youngest iPod family member: the iPod Touch. The Touch gets its moniker from its responsive *touch screen*, the smooth front side surface that lets you navigate through your music, videos, and photos with a tap or drag of your finger.

While it may have inherited its sensitivity from the iPhone, the Touch gets its stability from the same flash memory that's inside the Nano. No matter how hard you're running or rocking out, you'll probably never hear your music skip (something that's not always true with the spinning hard-drive based Classic). You get about 36 hours of audio playback on a battery charge—or 6 hours of video.

Speaking of video, the iPod Touch also has the iPhone's eye-catching 3.5-inch widescreen and 480 by 320 pixel resolution. Flip it sideways to see why it makes movies and TV shows look so good. Apple gives you three Touches to choose from: an 8-gigabyte model, a 16-gigabyte version, or one that can store 32 gigs of your favorite stuff. That's 1,750 songs or 10 hours of iPod-friendly video on the 8 GB Touch; 3,500 songs or 20 hours of video on the 16 GB model; and a nice healthy 7,000 songs and 40 hours of video on the big 32-gigabyte model.

But the iPod Touch is much more than just a pretty face. In addition to all its regular iPod capabilities, like listening to music or showing off your latest photos, this iPod can reach right out and touch the Internet. Thanks to a built-in Wi-Fi chip and a small-but-powerful version of Apple's Safari Web browser,

you can catch up on all the latest news whenever you're in range of a Wi-Fi network. You use your fingertips to point your way around the Web—or fire up the Touch's onscreen keyboard for when you have to enter text in a Web address or on a page.

And where there's Internet, there's email, stock-market updates, weather forecasts, and online maps. If that's not enough, there's a whole new world of possibilities in the iTunes App Store, where you can customize your iPod with additional software. Whether you're connected or not, you also get a handy notepad, your personal calendar, and your computer's address book, too.

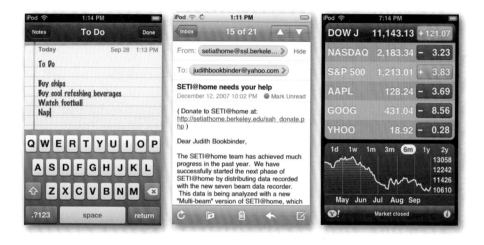

If you hate leaving your computer for fear of missing something totally cool posted on YouTube, the popular video-sharing site, the Touch is there for you. This wireless iPod comes with its own one-click link direct to YouTube so you can keep up with the Web's funniest videos.

Oh, and one more thing...have you ever been listening to your iPod and wished you could buy even more music right there, no matter where you are? With the Touch (and a wireless network connection), you can. This little Internet iPod can step right up to the iTunes Wi-Fi Music Store (Chapter 7) and search, sample, and snap up tracks over the airwaves.

Note They may look an awful lot alike, but the iPod Touch and the iPhone have some distinct differences. For one thing, the iPod Touch is not actually a mobile phone. While this means Touch owners get to skip the AT&T Experience, it also means there's no ubiquitous cellphone network to use for online fun when your pool of Wi-Fi hotspots runs cold. There's also no integrated 2-megapixel camera. On the plus side, without the extra hardware inside the Touch is much more svelte.

Install iTunes

Before you can have hours of iPod fun, you need to install the iTunes multi-media, multifunction jukebox program on your computer. With iTunes, you also get Apple's QuickTime software—a video helper for iTunes. iPods once came with a CD packing all these programs, but these days you have to download everything yourself:

❶ **Fire up your computer's Web browser and point it to** *www.apple.com/ipod/start.*

❷ **Click the "Download Now" button.** (Turn off the "Email me..." and "Keep me up to date..." checkboxes to spare yourself future marketing missives.) Wait for the file to download to your computer.

❸ **When the file lands on your hard drive, double-click the** *iTunes8Setup.exe* **file.** If you use a Mac, double-click the *iTunes.dmg* file and then open the *iTunes.mpkg* file to start the installation. But if your Mac's younger than six years old, you probably already have iTunes installed. Go to Menu→Software Update and ask your Mac to look for a newer version just in case.

❹ **Follow the screens until the software installer says it's done.**

You may need to restart your computer after the software's been installed. Once iTunes is loaded, you're ready to connect your new iPod to the computer.

Unpack iPod and Set It Up

If you haven't torn open the package already, liberate the iPod from its box. The items you'll find inside vary depending on which iPod you purchased, but all of them come with:

❶ The classic Apple white headphones.

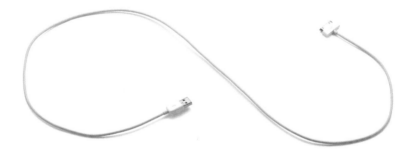

❷ A USB cable to connect the iPod to your computer. The iPod Classic, Nano, and Touch use the same white USB cable with the flat dock-connector port, while the iPod Shuffle has its own little USB dock.

❸ A little pamphlet of basic quick-start information that's not nearly as fun or as colorful as this book.

What you want right now is the USB cable. Connect the small, narrow end to your computer's USB port and the wide, flat end (or the dock, if you have a Shuffle) to the iPod. The first time you connect your iPod to a computer, the Setup Assistant walks you through a few steps to get your iPod ready to go.

The next step, if you want to hear some music, is to *get* some music on your iPod.

Three Ways to Get Music for iTunes (and iPod)

Once iTunes is installed on your computer, you can start filling it with music. Chapters 4 and 5 have info on digital audio formats and technical settings you can tweak, but if you've got a brand new iPod, odds are you don't care about *that* right now. No, you'd probably just like to get some music on your iPod. Here are three simple ways:

Import Existing Songs into iTunes

If you've had a computer for longer than a few years, odds are you already have some songs in the popular MP3 format already on your hard drive. When you start iTunes for the first time, the program asks if you'd like to search your Mac or PC for music and add it to iTunes. Click "Yes" and iTunes will go fetch.

iTunes Setup Assistant

Find Music Files

Would you like iTunes to search your Home folder for MP3 and AAC music files you already have? The songs will be copied into your iTunes Music folder so you can easily listen to them.

- ⦿ Yes, find MP3 and AAC files in my Home folder
- ○ No, I'll add them myself later

Cancel   Previous   Next

Note Now, many Windows fans, if they do have existing music, may have songs in the Windows Media Audio (WMA) format. The bad news here is that iTunes can't play WMA files. The good news is that iTunes, when it finds WMA files, can automatically convert them to an iPod-friendly format.

Import a CD

You can also use iTunes to convert tracks from your audio CDs into iPod-ready digital music files. Just stick a CD in your computer's disc drive after you start up iTunes. If you're connected to the Internet, iTunes automatically downloads song titles and artist information for the CD. The program asks if you want to import the CD into iTunes. (If it doesn't, just click the "Import CD" button at the bottom of the iTunes window.)

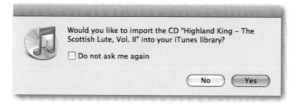

Once you tell it to import the music, iTunes gets to work and begins adding the songs to your library. You can import all the tracks from a CD, but if you don't want every song, then turn off the checkbox next to those titles and iTunes skips them. Chapter 4 has more about using iTunes to convert CDs.

Buy Music in the iTunes Store

Another way to get music for iPod and iTunes is to buy it from the iTunes Store. Click the iTunes Store icon in the list on the left side of iTunes. Once you land on the Store's main page and set up your iTunes account, you can buy and download songs, audio books, and videos. The content goes straight into your iTunes library and then onto your iPod. Chapter 7 is all about using the iTunes Store.

Get Stuff Onto the iPod Classic or Nano: The Quick Way

You don't have to do much to keep your music and video collection up to date between your computer and your iPod. That's because the iPod has a nifty *autosync* feature, which automatically makes sure that whatever's in your iTunes library also appears on your iPod once you connect it to the computer.

The first time you plug in your new iPod (after you've installed iTunes, of course), the iPod Setup Assistant leaps into action, asks you to name your iPod, and asks if you'd like to "Automatically sync songs to my iPod". If your answer's "yes," just click the Finish button. iTunes loads a copy of everything in its library onto your iPod. That's it. Your iPod's ready to go.

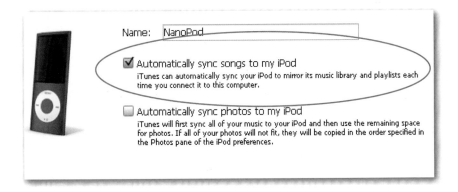

You can also copy over photos from your computer here, too. But if you just want to stick with the music for now, Chapter 9 can fill you in on the photo business. If you generally like autosync but want more control over what goes onto the iPod, read on to find out how to make that happen.

> **Note** If you have an iPod Shuffle, you may already have more music than can fit on the small player. If that's the case, *your* automatic option is the Autofill button at the bottom of the iTunes window. Skip ahead to page 14 to learn more about Autofill, which lets iTunes decide what to put on your Shuffle. If you want to be the boss of your Shuffle's music, page 15 has instructions.

Manually Load the iPod Classic or Nano

If you don't have enough room on your Classic or Nano for your whole iTunes collection, or plan to load music onto your iPod from more than one computer (say your work and home PCs), you'll want to *manually manage* your songs and other stuff. To put your iPod on manual right from the get-go turn off the checkbox on the iPod Setup Assistant screen next to "Automatically sync songs..." (If you've already done the Setup Thing, see page 106 for how to come back to Manual Land.) iTunes now refrains from automatically dumping everything onto your iPod. "But," you ask, "*How* do I get the music on there by myself?" It's easy. You just drag it:

❶ **In iTunes, click the Music icon under Library.** You see an array of album covers; double-click one to view its list of tracks. You can also click the button circled below to go into iTunes List view. Press Ctrl+B (⌘-B) to get the full display of Genre, Artist, Album, and Song lists.

❷ **Click the album name, cover, or songs you want to copy to the iPod.** Grab multiple song titles or albums by holding down the Control or ⌘ key.

❸ **Drag your selection onto the iPod icon.** The number of songs you're dragging appears inside a red circle.

You can manually place any items in your iTunes library—audio books, movies, whatever—onto your iPod this way.

Get Songs on the iPod Shuffle Quickly

Most people's entire music library is too big to stuff onto the wee Shuffle, but you can Autofill it with a Shuffle-sized serving of tunes. If this is the first time you're plugging your player into the computer, the iPod Setup Assistant appears. Leave the "Automatically choose songs..." checkbox turned on, click Done, and presto: iTunes grabs a collection of songs from your library and copies them onto your Shuffle. After that, each time you connect your tiny Pod, a small panel appears at the bottom of iTunes, inviting you to fill up your iPod with the click of the Autofill button.

iTunes can snag songs from your entire library or just a particular playlist (see Chapter 6); you can also opt to have iTunes select highly rated songs more often. ("Ratings?" you say? Check out Chapter 5 for the details.)

The Autofill box also has a setting called "Choose items randomly." Turning this checkbox on means iTunes moves over songs in whatever order it feels like, instead of transferring them in the same order they appear in the iTunes Library or a selected playlist.

Once you've Autofilled for the first time and then return for another batch of songs, you can turn on the checkbox next to "Replace all items when Autofilling" to have iTunes wipe the first batch of songs off the Shuffle and substitute new tracks.

Once iTunes has filled up the Shuffle, you'll see the "iPod sync is complete" message at the top of iTunes. Click the Eject button next to your Shuffle's icon, and then unplug the player from the computer.

Manually Load the iPod Shuffle

If you want to decide what goes on your Shuffle, you can opt for manual updating instead of letting iTunes choose. As with any other iPod on manual control, you can drag songs and playlists from your iTunes library and drop them on the Shuffle's icon in the Source list.

When you've clicked the Shuffle's icon, feel free to arrange individual songs into the order you want to hear them—just drag them up or down. The info down at the bottom of the iTunes window tells you how much space you've got left on your Shuffle if you're looking to fill it to the rim. To delete songs from the Shuffle, just select one or more tracks and then press the Delete key on your keyboard.

You can also mix and match your song-loading methods. Start by dragging a few favorite playlists over to the Shuffle, and then click Autofill to finish the job. Just make sure the "Replace all items when Autofilling" checkbox isn't turned on or iTunes will wipe off all those tracks you personally added.

While regular hard drive iPods set to manual update can collect songs from multiple computers—say, your work and home PCs—the stubborn Shuffle is monogamous and demands to be associated with only one computer.

Get Stuff on the iPod Touch: The Quick Way

As with every iPod model that's come before it, the iPod Touch offers the simple and effective autosync feature. Autosyncing automatically puts a copy of every song, podcast, and video in your iTunes library right onto your player. In fact, the first time you connect your iPod Touch to your computer, the iPod Setup Assistant offers to copy all the music in your iTunes library over to your new player. If you opted to do that, your iPod is already set for autosync.

If you've added more music since that first encounter, the steps for loading the new goods onto your Touch couldn't be easier:

❶ Plug the USB cable into your Windows PC or Macintosh.

❷ Plug the flat end of that same USB cable into the bottom of the iPod Touch.

❸ Sit back and let iTunes leap into action, syncing away and doing all that heavy lifting for you.

You can tell the sync magic is working because iTunes gives you a progress report at the top of its window that says "Syncing iPod Touch..." (or whatever you've named your player. When iTunes tells you the iPod's update is complete, you're free to unplug your Touch and take off.

Autosync is a beautiful thing, but it's not for everyone—especially if you have more than 8-, 16-, or 32-gigabytes worth of stuff in your iTunes library. (That may sound like a lot of room for music, but once you start adding hefty video files, that space disappears fast.)

If autosync isn't for you, jump over to the next page to read about more selective ways to load up your Touch.

Manually Load the iPod Touch

If you opt out of autosyncing your iPod Touch, you now need to go ahead and choose some songs for it. Until you do, the Touch just sits there empty and forlorn in your iTunes window, waiting for you to give it something to play with.

Manual method #1

❶ Click the iPod Touch icon on the left side of the iTunes window. This opens up a world of syncing preferences for getting stuff on your iPod.

❷ Click the Music tab, then turn on the "Sync Music" checkbox.

❸ Click the button next to "Selected playlists" and check off the names of the iTunes playlists you want to copy to your iPod. (Don't have any playlists yet? See Chapter 6.)

❹ Click the Apply button at the bottom of the iTunes window.

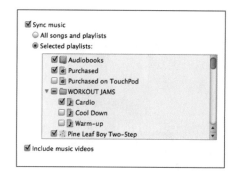

Manual method #2

❶ This one's for those into fine-grained picking and choosing: Click the Summary tab and turn on "Manually manage music and videos." Now you can click the songs, albums, or playlists you want and drag them to the Touch icon in the iTunes Source pane.

Manual method #3

❶ Every item in your iTunes library has a checkmark next to its name when you first import it. Clear that checkmark next to whatever you *don't* want on the Touch. (If you have a big library, hold down the Control [⌘] key while clicking any title; that performs the nifty trick of removing all checkmarks. Then go check the stuff you *do* want.)

❷ Click the iPod Touch icon under Devices on the left side of the iTunes window, and then click the Summary tab.

❸ At the bottom of the Summary screen, turn on the checkbox next to "Sync only checked songs and videos" and then click the Sync button.

Disconnect the iPod from Your Computer

Got iTunes installed? *Check.*

Got music in the iTunes library? *Check.*

Got the iPod connected and the music you want copied onto it? *Check.*

Next up: Disconnect the iPod from your computer so you can enjoy your tunes. Resist the impulse to yank the USB cable out of the iPod without checking the iPod's screen first. If the iPod is showing its menus or the battery icon, then you can safely unplug it.

But if you see the image shown at left, you need to *manually* eject the iPod from your computer. iTunes gives you two easy ways to do this:

❶ Click the little Eject icon next to the name of your iPod in the iTunes Source list.

❷ If your iPod's already selected in the Source list, choose Control→Eject iPod or press Ctrl+E (⌘-E).

With either method, the iPod's screen announces it's ejecting and displays an "OK to Disconnect" progress bar as it breaks its connection with the computer. Once all the gray screens go away and you see the regular menus again, you can safely liberate your iPod.

Charge the iPod the First Time

Right out of the box, your iPod's battery probably has enough juice to run for a little while without having to charge it up. Eventually, though, you'll need to go in for an electrical fill up. All you need to do is plug the iPod back into your computer with the USB cable (the iPod charges itself by drawing from your Mac or PC's power). Just make sure the computer is turned on and isn't asleep.

It takes only a few hours to fully charge your iPod's battery, and even less time to do what Apple calls a *fast charge*, which fills up 80 percent of the battery's capacity. That should be plenty of gas in your iPod's tank for a quick spin.

Here's how much time each type of iPod needs for both a fast- and a full-charge:

	Fast Charge	Full Charge
iPod Classic	2 hours	4 hours
iPod Nano	1.5 hours	3 hours
iPod Shuffle	2 hours	4 hours
iPod Touch	2 hours	4 hours

If you're traveling and don't want to drag your laptop with you just to charge your iPod, you can buy an AC adapter for it. Chapter 2 has more information on that.

Control the iPod Classic or Nano with the Click Wheel

Smack in the iPod's belly is the *click wheel,* your way around the iPod's contents. It's called a click wheel because you can actually click down on the four buttons evenly arranged around the ring. The menus on screen spin by as your thumb moves around the circle. There's also a big button in the wheel's center, which you'll be pushing a lot as you use your iPod. Here's what each button does, going clockwise from the top.

❶ **Menu.** Tap this button to return to any screen you've just viewed. For example, if you've visited Music→Playlists→My Top Rated, then press Menu twice to return to the Music menu. If you keep tapping Menu, you eventually wind up on the main iPod menu.

❷ **Fast-forward/Next.** Press this button to jump to the next song in a playlist (Chapter 6), or hold it down to advance quickly within a song.

❸ **Play/Pause.** Just like on a CD player, this button starts a song; push it again to pause the music.

❹ **Rewind/Previous.** Press this button to play the song directly before the current track (or hold it down to "rewind" within a song).

❺ **Select.** Like clicking a mouse button, press Select to choose a highlighted menu item. When a song title is highlighted, the Select button also begins playback.

Other iPod Ports and Switches

On the outside, the iPod isn't a very complicated device. There's really just a Hold switch and two jacks to plug in cords. Here's what you do with 'em.

❶ **Hold Switch.** At the top of the Classic, over on the left side, is a little sliding switch marked Hold. This is a control that deactivates all the iPod's front buttons. Turning on the Hold switch stops your iPod from popping on if the buttons accidentally get bumped. The Nano's tiny Hold button is also on the top-left edge; the Touch doesn't have a Hold button, since it locks its screen when you press its Sleep/Wake button on top.

❷ **Headphone Jack.** Your new iPod comes with its own bright white headphones, and they plug in right here. If you don't like Apple's headphones, you can use another style or brand, as long as the other headphones use the standard 3.5-millimeter stereo miniplug.

❸ **Dock Connector.** The flat port on the iPod's bottom is called the Dock Connector. This is where you plug in the USB cable so you can connect iPod to a computer for battery-charging and music- and video-fill ups. (The Nano's headphone jack is also on the bottom.)

Basic Finger Moves for the iPod Touch Screen

Until the iPhone and the iPod Touch arrived on the scene, iPods were controlled by a wheel or control ring on the front of the player. The Classic, the Nano, and the Shuffle still work that way, but if you have an iPod Touch, you don't need a steering wheel to get around the iPod—you just tap the icons and menus directly on the screen to navigate around the device.

There are four moves you'll use most often when navigating the Touch screen:

- **Tap.** Just take the tip of your finger and directly touch the icon, song title, or control you see on the screen. The iPod Touch is not a crusty old calculator, so you don't have to push very hard. A gentle press will do.

- **Drag.** Keep your fingertip pressed down on the screen and slide it around to scroll around to different parts of the screen. You can do things like move volume sliders on music tracks or scoot over to different parts of a photo by dragging.

- **Flick.** Lightly and quickly whip your finger up or down a vertical list of songs on the iPod Touch screen, and watch them whiz by in the direction you flicked. The faster you flick that finger, the faster the text on screen scrolls by. You can also flick side-to-side in Cover Flow view (Chapter 3) or in a photo album to see images parade triumphantly across your screen.

- **Slide.** A slide is sort of like a drag, but you mainly do it when you're presented with a special button on screen, like unlocking the iPod Touch's main screen when you first turn it on.

Note The iPod Touch relies on the human touch—skin-on-glass contact—to work. If you have really long fingernails, a Band-Aid on the tip of your finger, or happen to be wearing gloves, you're going to have problems working the iPod Touch. You also can't use a pencil eraser or pen tip, either.

Special Buttons on the iPod Touch

The iPod Touch has the same headphone port on top and dock-connector jack on the bottom like other iPods. But because most of its controls are behind its sensitive screen, the iPod Touch only has a couple of physical buttons on the outside.

One of these is the volume rocker on the left side. Pressing the top nib increases the sound on either the tiny little external speaker or an attached pair of headphones; the bottom nib lowers the volume.

For your pushing pleasure, the Touch comes with two other buttons:

- **Home.** Forget clicking your heels together three times—just push this indented button on the bottom of the Touch and you'll always return home. The iPod's Home screen is where all your tappable icons for Music, Photos, Safari, and more all hang out. If you ever wander deep into the iPod and don't know how to get out, push the Home button to escape. You can also push it to wake up the iPod Touch from sleep.

- **Sleep/Wake.** Press the thin black button on top of the Touch to put it to sleep and save some battery power. If you've got a song playing, no problem: a sleeping Touch still plays—it's just the display that goes dark.

Find the Music on Your iPod—
and Play It

Now that you've got some songs on the iPod, you're ready to listen to them. Plug your headphones into the headphone jack and press any button on the front of the iPod if you need to turn it on.

Find Music on Your Classic or Nano

After you pick a language, the first menu you see says iPod at the top of the screen. Here's how to start playing your tunes:

❶ **On the iPod menu, highlight the Music menu.** Run your thumb over the scroll wheel to move the blue highlight bar up and down.

❷ **Press the round center button to select Music.**

❸ **On the Music menu, scroll to whichever category you want to use to find your song.** Your choices include Artist, Album, Song, Genre, and so on. Scroll to the one you want and press the center button to see your songs sorted by your chosen method.

```
Music
  Genius
  Playlists
  Artists                >
  Albums
  Songs
  Genres
  Composers
  Audiobooks
  Search
```

❹ **Scroll through the list on the iPod's screen.** Say you decided to look for music by Artist. You now see a list of all the singers and bands stored on your iPod. Scroll down to the one you want and press the center button. A list of all the albums you have from that artist appears on screen.

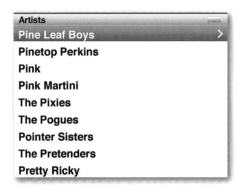

❺ Scroll to the one you want to hear. Press the Play/Pause button to start playing the album.

You can find anything on your iPod by scrolling around and pressing the center button to select the item you want to hear, watch, read, or play. If you end up on a screen where you don't want to be, then press the Menu button to retrace your steps. In fact, you can keep pressing the Menu button to reverse course and go all the way back to the iPod's main menu.

Press the Play/Pause button to pause a song that's playing. If a song's not playing and you don't touch the iPod's buttons for a few minutes, it puts itself to sleep automatically to save battery power.

Find Music on Your iPod Touch

"Hey!" you say, "I have an iPod Touch! How do I find my music since I don't have a scroll wheel?" Here's what you do.

❶ Tap the Music button on the Home screen.

❷ At the bottom of the Music screen are five tappable buttons. These let you see your music sorted by Playlists, Artists, Songs, or Albums. (There's also a More button at the end that lets you sort by Genre, Compilation, and other categories.)

❸ Tap the Songs button and then scroll (by flicking your finger) down to the song you want to play. You can also hold down the alphabet bar on the right and then slide your finger slowly to better control the scroll. Tap the song's title to hear it play.

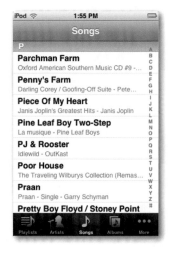

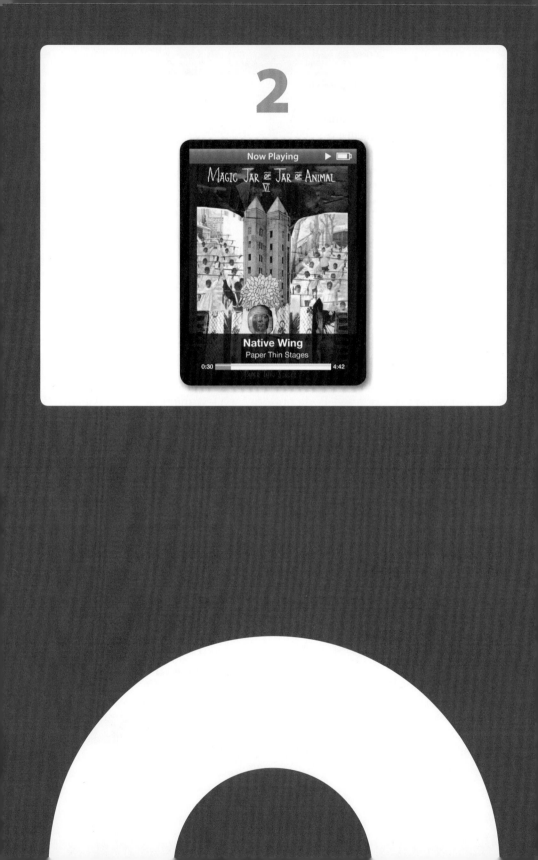

Bopping Around the iPod Classic, Nano, and Shuffle

T he standard iPod is a very simple device to operate—five buttons and a click wheel quickly take you to all your songs, movies, games, audio books, and everything else parked on your 'Pod. Even though it doesn't have a mouse, the player's controls work just like a desktop computer: you highlight an item onscreen and click the center button to select it.

Performing this action either takes you to another menu of options or starts a function—like playing a song, calling up your calendar, or checking the time in Paris. This chapter shows you what lies underneath all the menus on your iPod Classic or Nano and what each item does. Shuffle owners will find special coverage of their screenless wonders sprinkled throughout the chapter. The iPod Touch, unique among iPods for its lack of buttons and wheel-free controls, gets its own chapter right after this one.

Turn the iPod On and Off— or Put It On Hold

Classic or Nano, the iPod has only five buttons and one switch—and none of them are labeled Off or On. It's not hard to do either, even without official buttons.

- To turn the iPod on, just tap any button on the front and it wakes right up, ready to play music or movies.

- To turn the iPod off, press the Play/Pause button for a few seconds until the screen goes off. To preserve battery power, an inactive iPod automatically shuts itself down after a couple of minutes.

- For a one-click trip to Naptown from the iPod's main menu, add the Sleep option to the list. Choose iPod→Settings→Main Menu→Sleep. (On the Nano, that's iPod→Settings→General→Main Menu→Sleep.)

However, if its front buttons get bumped, say, in a purse or backpack, the iPod can turn on and run its battery down without you knowing it. Then you end up with a drained iPod right before that long commute home.

That's where the **Hold switch** on the iPod comes in handy. It's on the top of the Classic, the current Nano, and older iPods. (On older Nanos it's on the bottom.) Just slide it over so the orange bit underneath shows, and your iPod's front buttons are deactivated and won't respond to inadvertent taps. Flicking the Hold switch is good for preventing accidental battery drains; it's great if you have the iPod in your pocket and don't want to jump to the next song every time you inadvertently graze the click wheel.

> **Note** Keeping the iPod Shuffle from accidentally turning on is simple: just flick the bottom-side's right-hand switch to Off. But what if you're playing music and want to temporarily disable the front-side buttons—for example, so you don't inadvertently pump up the volume or switch tracks? Just press the Play/Pause button for three seconds to toggle a kind of virtual Hold mode off or on. If you later press the Play button and get three blinks of amber light, the Shuffle's telling you it's on Hold. Press Play/Pause again for three seconds to unlock it—three blinks of the green light means Hold is off.

Navigate the iPod's Menus

Like any modern computer program, the iPod's user interface is made up of a series of menus and sub-menus. The top-level, or main menu, just says iPod at the top of the screen. No matter how deeply you burrow into the player's submenus, you can always get back to the main menu by repeatedly pressing the Menu button on the click wheel.

In fact, think of iPod navigation like this: Press the round center button to go deeper into the menus and press the Menu button to back out and retrace your steps.

The contents of your iPod menu varies a bit depending on which model you have—except for the Shuffle, of course, which doesn't have a screen or menus. Here's the basic lineup if you have a song currently playing:

- **Music**
- **Videos**
- **Photos**
- **Podcasts**

- **Extras**
- **Settings**
- **Shuffle Songs**
- **Now Playing**

The next few pages give you a little more information about each menu. And just as the iPod and iTunes give you choices about your music, you can also decide for yourself what you want displayed on your main menu. If you like the sound of that, check out "Customize Your iPod's Menus" later in this chapter.

What's in the Music Menu

In the Music menu you'll find a one-stop shopping center for your iPod's audio-related options, including tunes, audio books, and podcasts.

- **Cover Flow.** A feature so cool, it gets its own page, over there on the right. (Only the Classic menu actually lists this item, as the Nano has its own shortcut to it.)

- **Genius.** Instructions on how to use your iPod's very own mixmaster. Chapter 6 explains the genius of Genius in greater detail.

- **Playlists.** A *playlist* is a customized list of songs you create. Chapter 6 has loads more info on creating playlists.

- **Artists.** This menu groups every tune by the performer's name.

- **Albums.** Your music, grouped by album.

- **Songs.** All the songs on your iPod, listed alphabetically.

- **Genres.** Your music, sorted by type: rock, rap, country, and so on.

- **Composers.** Your music, grouped by songwriter.

- **Audiobooks.** Your iPod's spoken-word content.

- **Search.** When you have a ton of tunes and don't feel like scrolling through your collection, use the Search function to scroll-and-click the first few letters using a tiny onscreen keyboard. Songs that match pop up in their own list.

Even without using the Search function, the Music menu's sub-menus make it easy to find specific music. For example, to see a list of all songs on your iPod sorted by artist, select Artists from the Music menu. The next screen presents you with an alphabetical list of bands and singers.

Music
Genius
Playlists
Artists ❯
Albums
Songs
Genres
Composers
Audiobooks
Search

Cover Flow on the iPod

The iPod offers a number of ways for you to browse your music collection, like scrolling through lists grouped by artist, album, or song. But if you want to see all your album covers majestically parade across your screen, choose iPod→Music→Cover Flow (on the Classic), and then turn the scroll wheel. On the Nano, just hold the iPod sideways in "landscape" view to switch to Cover Flow.

Cover Flow on the iPod looks pretty much like the Cover Flow view in iTunes (Chapter 4), except for some reason, it actually looks *cooler* on the iPod. It's also quite helpful to see what songs you have from each particular album sliding by. Here's how:

When the cover of the album you want to hear appears in the center of the iPod's screen, press the Select button. The artwork animatedly flips around to reveal the track names and times for each song from the selected album. Scroll down the list and click the Select button again to play the chosen song.

If you don't have any artwork attached to your music files, Cover Flow can be a little bland because it just displays a default gray music-note icon. Flip to Chapter 5 if you want to get a rolling start building up your art collection.

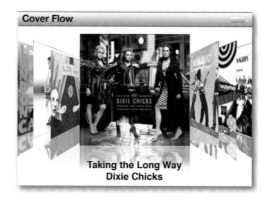

What's in the Videos Menu

Your iPod is also a personal movie player. Before you grab the popcorn, here's what you'll find on its menu of video-setting and sorting options:

- **Movies.** Go here to find any full-length feature films you've purchased from the iTunes Store as well as your own home movies.

- **Rentals.** If you opted to rent a movie instead of buying it outright, you'll find it waiting for you in this menu.

- **TV Shows.** A menu for iTunes Store-purchased episodes and personally recorded shows.

- **Music Videos.** A list of your collected music video clips.

- **Video Playlists.** Just like music, you can create playlists of videos in iTunes.

- **Settings.** You can configure your TV playback options. For example, you can set the iPod to play video in widescreen format or adjust it for full-screen viewing. An option to turn on closed-captioning is here, too.

Playing a video works just like playing a song: browse, scroll, and select. Chapters 7 and 8 tell you how to buy, sort, and organize your iPod's video collection using iTunes.

What's in the Photos Menu

Ready to turn your iPod into a pocket photo viewer? Once you stock your iPod with images (Chapter 9 has instructions), the Photos menu lets you adjust picture-viewing preferences—including slideshow settings for picture collections—and call up your actual pix.

All Photos

Click here to view your iPod's entire photo library; individual albums are listed by name below the Settings menu. Chapter 9 shows you how to summon your pictures onscreen.

Settings

- **Time Per Slide.** Linger up to 20 seconds on each photo or manually click through each picture.

- **Music.** Select a playlist as your soundtrack, or choose silence.

- **Repeat.** As with playlists, slideshows can repeat—if you want 'em to.

- **Shuffle Photos.** Toggle the setting to On to randomly display each photo in a slideshow.

- **Transitions.** Options here include a classic Hollywood fade, a dissolve, and many more.

- **TV Out.** To display your slideshow on a connected TV, select On or Ask. For slideshows on the iPod, choose Off or Ask. (Off does what it says; Ask nags you to pick between TV and iPod before the show starts.) Nano and Classic owners only get the Off setting till they've actually plugged in a video-ready cable.

- **TV Signal.** When using a TV in North or South America, or East Asia, select NTSC; most other places use the PAL standard.

What's in the Podcasts Menu

When podcasts first appeared online several years ago, they were mostly audio files: radio-like shows to download and play on your iPod. But podcasts are not just about audio these days—there are plenty of video podcasts out there for the watching too. If you want to dive in and go get some shows right now, Chapter 7 explains how to download and subscribe to podcasts from the iTunes Store.

There are a couple of really great things about podcasts. For one, pretty much all of them are still free, so you have a wealth of fresh content available to put on your iPod every day. And another thing: They've become so popular that they rate their own menu on the latest iPod models.

Go to iPod→Podcasts to see the shows you've downloaded and synced up through iTunes. On the iPod's menu, the podcasts are sorted by the name of the show, like *BBC Digital Planet* or *Ask a Ninja*, with the total number of episodes on the iPod listed. If you haven't yet listened to an episode, a blue dot appears next to the name—which makes it easy to find the new stuff.

What's in the Extras Menu

Here lie all the goodies that make the iPod more than just a music player:

- **Alarms.** Have the iPod wake you up with a beep—or put you to sleep with a timer setting that lets you drift off to Dreamland with music.

- **Calendars.** This menu holds a copy of your personal daily schedule from iCal or Microsoft Outlook.

- **Clocks.** With its built-in clock and ability to display multiple different time zones, the iPod is probably the most stylish pocket watch you'll ever see.

- **Contacts.** Any phone numbers and addresses you've ported over from your computer reside here.

- **Games.** Test your capacity for trivia with iQuiz, kill time with a round of Klondike solitaire, or shoot things in the Vortex. Games from the iTunes Store, like Ms. Pac-Man and Sudoku, also land here.

- **Notes.** The iPod has a built-in text reader program that you can use to read short documents and notes.

- **Screen Lock.** With all your stuff that's nobody's business—address book, schedule, photos, etc.—you may want to password protect your 'Pod.

- **Stopwatch.** The iPod can serve as your timer for keeping track of your overall workout or multiple laps around the track.

Check out Chapter 10 for more information on turning your iPod into a time-keeper, a handheld organizer, and more.

Note The Classic and the Nano show these menu items in a slightly different order. The Nano goes for the alphabetical approach listed in the text above.

What's in the Settings Menu

The Settings menu has more than a dozen options for tailoring your iPod's look and sound.

- **About.** Look here for your iPod's serial number; the number of songs, videos, and photos on it; your model's hard drive size; and how much free disk space is left. Click the center button to see all three screens of info.

- **Shuffle.** Turn this feature on to shuffle songs or albums.

- **Repeat.** Repeat One plays the current song over and over; Repeat All repeats the current album, playlist, or song library.

- **EQ.** Apply more than 20 different equalizer presets for acoustic, classical, hip hop, and other types of music. Chapter 5 has more on equalization.

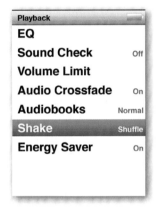

- **Sound Check.** Turning on Sound Check helps level out songs of differing volumes. Chapter 5 has more info.

- **Volume Limit.** Keep your (or your child's) eardrums from melting by setting a maximum volume limit—and locking it.

- **Audio Crossfade.** On the Nano, turning this setting on means never having to hear a gap between songs as the iPod fades out of one tune and into the next.

- **Audiobooks.** This setting lets you speed up or slow down the narrator's voice.

- **Shake.** Put this setting to Shuffle on the Nano. Then give it a gentle shake the next time you're playing a song and want to change randomly to another track. The Nano emits a booping tone and serves up a new tune.

- **Energy Saver.** This feature turns off the Nano's screen if you're not currently pressing the iPod buttons—and saves you a little battery juice.

> **Note** The Nano groups the music-oriented settings like EQ, Sound Check, and Audio Crossfade into a Playback submenu on the main Settings menu. Other settings like Clicker, Backlight, and Main Menu—all the stuff that lets you fuss with the look and sound of the Nano text screens—are grouped under the General submenu.

- **Clicker.** Some people think the Clicker noise during a long scroll sounds like ants tap dancing. Others like the audio cue. Decide for yourself and turn the sound off or on here.

- **Backlight.** Specify how long the backlight stays on each time you press a button or turn the dial—from 2 Seconds to Always On.

- **Brightness.** If your iPod movies seem a bit dim (and not just because of Hollywood's standards), use this setting to brighten the screen.

- **Font Size.** On the Nano, you can make the tiny screen type slightly bigger by switching from Standard to Large.

- **Main Menu.** Customize which items appear in your iPod's main menu here.

- **Music Menu.** Customize which items appear in the Music menu here, like Radio—for when you have Apple's optional FM Radio Remote.

- **Sort Contacts.** This setting for your Contacts lets you change the sorting order of the first and last names of people in your iPod's address book.

- **Date & Time.** Adjust your iPod's date, time, and time zone settings here.

- **Language.** The iPod can display its menus in most major European and Asian languages. Pick one here.

- **Legal.** The Legal menu contains a long scroll of copyright notices for Apple and its software partners. It's not very interesting reading unless perhaps you're studying intellectual-property law.

- **Reset All Settings.** This command returns all your iPod's customized sound and display settings back to their original factory settings.

Other Menus: Shuffle Songs and Now Playing

One—sometimes two—other items live down at the bottom of the iPod's main menu.

Shuffle Songs

The mystical, magical qualities of the iPod's Shuffle Songs setting (*"How does my little PeaPod always know when to play my Weird Al Yankovic and Monty Python songs to cheer me up?"*) have become one of the player's most popular features since the early days of iPodding. So Apple moved Shuffle out to the main menu. Just scroll and select if you want to shuffle your songs.

Now Playing

When you have a song playing—but have scrolled back to the main menu to do something else while jamming—the Now Playing item appears at the very bottom of the screen. Highlight this command and press Select to call up your song's Now Playing screen and get back to the music at hand.

Press the iPod's center button quickly when you're on the Now Playing screen to get a new mini-menu each time you hit the button, like the scrubber bar (page 43) or the chance to rate the song (Chapter 5).

Customize Your iPod's Menus

The iPod has a handy personalization feature: the ability to arrange both your Main Menu and Music Menu screens so that only the items you like show up there. For example, you could insert the Calendar option onto the iPod's main screen so that you don't have to dig through the Extras menu to get at it. Or put your Playlists menu right out there on the main screen so you don't waste time getting to your latest musical inspiration.

To customize your Nano's main menu, start from the main iPod screen and choose Settings→General→Main Menu. On the iPod Classic, go to Settings→Main Menu. You see a list of items that you can choose to add or eliminate from the main screen: Music, Playlists, Artists, and so on.

Main Menu	
Preview Panel	On
Music	✔
Genius	
Playlists	✔
Artists	
Albums	
Compilations	
Songs	
Genres	
Composers	

As you scroll down the list, press the center button to turn each one on or off. You might, for example, consider adding these commands:

• **Clock,** for quick checks of the time.

• **Games,** for quick killing of time.

• **Contacts,** to look up phone numbers and call people to pass the time.

To see the fruits of your labor, press Menu twice to return to the main screen. Sure enough, in addition to the usual commands described in this chapter, you'll see the formerly buried menus right out front, ready to go.

Now that you've got your Main Menu screen squared away, you can do the same type of customization on your iPod's Music screen by choosing Settings→Music Menu.

> **Tip** You can see more menu items and less eye candy on the skinny Nano's main screen by turning off the Preview Panel—that strip of images at the bottom of the window. Choose Settings→General→Main Menu→Preview Panel→Off. Your menu response time will get a lot peppier, too. As of now, the Classic's wider preview panel stays put on the right side of the screen.

Set the iPod's Clock(s)

When you choose Clocks from the iPod's Extras menu, you can set up live clocks tracking multiple cities. This little timekeeper comes in handy if you forget your watch.

- To create a clock, choose Clocks and press the iPod's center button. A box appears with a choice of Add or Edit. Scroll to Add and click the center button to select it.

- To change the location of an existing clock, click it with the iPod's center button and then select Edit. Pick the general region you want from the Region menu; then choose the new city on the next screen.

- To delete a clock from the list, select it, press the center button, and choose Delete.

- To make adjustments for things like Daylight Saving Time, the date, the time zone—or to opt for the military-style 24-hour clock display— choose iPod→Settings→Date & Time.

> **Tip** You can ask the iPod to display the current time in its title bar whenever music's playing. Just choose iPod→Settings→Date & Time→"Time in Title". Press the center button to toggle the "Time in Title" display on or off.

Use the iPod as an Alarm Clock

The alarm clock can give you a gentle nudge when you need it. To set your iPod's alarm:

❶ **Choose Extras→Alarms→Create Alarm. Press the center button.** The Alarm changes to On and you land on a screen full of choices.

❷ **Choose Date.** As you turn the wheel, you change the date for your wake-up call. Press the center button as you pick the month, day, minutes, and so on.

❸ **Choose Time.** Repeat the wheel-turning and clicking to choose the hour, minute, and AM/PM setting for the alarm. When you get back to the Create Alarm menu, click Repeat if this is a standing alert. Choose the alarm's frequency: daily, weekly, and so on.

❹ **Choose Sound.** It's time to decide whether you want "Beep" (a warbling R2-D2-like noise that comes out of the iPod's built-in speaker) or music. If you choose music, it plays through your headphones, assuming they haven't fallen out—or an external set of speakers if you have some.

❺ **Choose Label.** What's alarming you—class, a meeting, time to take a pill? Pick a name for your alarm here.

If you wake up early and want to turn off the alarm, go to Extras→Alarms→ [Name of Alarm]→Alarm and press the center button to toggle it off. You can also delete any alarm with the Delete option at the bottom of the menu.

Search for Songs on the iPod

As your music collection grows, scrolling to find a specific song or album can leave your thumb weary. Sometimes, you may not even remember if you *have* a certain song on the iPod. The Search feature, available on iPods released in the past few years, lets you drill down through your massive library and locate specific songs, albums, and so on with a few spins of the click wheel. It works like this:

❶ Choose iPod→Music→Search.

❷ On the screen that appears, use the click wheel to highlight a letter from the alphabet. Press the center button to select a letter.

❸ The iPod immediately presents a list of narrowed down matching titles, winnowing it further as you select more letters. Use the iPod's Rewind/ Previous key as a Backspace to wipe out letters you don't want.

❹ Once the title you want appears onscreen, click the Menu button (to jump up to the results list) and then scroll down to select your pick.

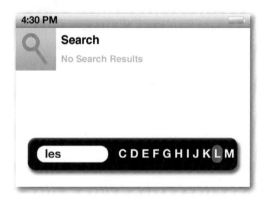

Tip iPod Shuffle owners, this one's just for you: To jump back to the very first song on your Shuffle's playlist, flip the shuffle switch to Play In Order (which looks like two arrows chasing each other's tails). Then click the Play/Pause button three times fast.

Jump Around Within Songs and Videos

Sometimes, you just have to hear the good part again or watch that scene in the movie once more because it was so cool the first time. If that's the case, the iPod gives you the controls to do so.

Hold down the Rewind/Previous and the Fast-forward/Next buttons on either side of the click wheel to zip back and forth through the song or video clip.

If you want to get to a specific time in the song or video, press the iPod's center button and then use the wheel to scroll over to the exact spot in the track's onscreen timeline. For an audio file, a small diamond appears in the timeline when you press the center button so you can see where you are in the song.

This jump-to-the-best-part technique is called *scrubbing*, so if a fellow iPodder tells you to scrub over to 2:05 in the song to hear that great guitar solo, the person's not talking about cleaning the bathtub.

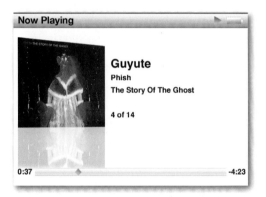

Tip If you find the iPod's backlight doesn't stay on nearly as long as you'd like, you can change the amount of time it shines. Choose Settings→General→Backlight (on the Nano), or Settings→Backlight (on the Classic). Scroll to the amount of time you'd like to see the light: increments between 2 and 30 seconds, or Always On. That last one's a real battery killer, though, as all that illumination needs power.

Adjust the iPod's Volume

The control ring on the iPod Shuffle has plus (+) and minus (–) buttons to pump up (or down) your music's volume. The volume knob on the larger iPods is virtual. With the song or video playing, run your thumb over the click wheel; the timeline bar on the bottom switches to a volume-level indicator.

If you want to protect your hearing, use the Volume Limit setting to lock in a maximum volume of your own choosing. Parents who worry that their kids are blasting music too loudly can set a Volume Limit and lock it with a numeric password:

❶ Go to iPod→Settings→Volume Limit (on the Classic), or iPod→Settings→General→Volume Limit (on the Nano).

❷ On the next screen, use the click wheel to select the highest volume level you want to have on the volume bar.

❸ Press the Play/Pause button to set it and to move to the next screen. (On the Nano, press the center button and choose either Done or Lock on the next screen. If you pick Lock, the next step is for you.)

❹ The iPod's Screen Lock display appears and you can dial in a secret four-number password that must be entered again to change the setting.

> **Tip** Need some soothing sounds at the end of a long day—but don't want the iPod on all night if you drift off? Have it sing you to sleep with the Sleep Timer function. Choose Extras→Alarms→Sleep Timer and then pick the amount of time you'd like: 15, 30, 60, 90, or 120 minutes. (You can also choose to turn the timer off here as well). Once you've picked your time, press Play and relax. The Sleep Timer item in the Alarms menu displays a countdown of time left, but hopefully, you'll be too sleepy to look.

Charge the iPod Without the Computer

The USB 2.0 cable (or USB Dock, if you have a Shuffle) that comes with your iPod has two jobs:

* To connect your iPod to iTunes.

* To draw power from the computer to charge up the iPod's battery.

There may be times, however, when your iPod's battery is in the red and you're nowhere near your computer. You many not even be near an electrical outlet, but on the road. Then it's time to turn to other options, including:

* **Using an Apple iPod USB Power Adapter.** This white box has a jack to plug in your iPod's USB cable (and connected iPod) into the back end. The adapter has a set of silver power prongs that flip up and plug into a regular electrical outlet. You can find the AC adapter for around $29 in iPod-friendly stores or online at *http://store.apple.com*.

* **Getting a car charger that connects to the standard 12-volt power outlet found in most cars.** Several companies make auto chargers for the iPod for around $20, and you can find the hardware at stores that sell iPod gear, Apple Stores (including *http://store.apple.com*) and specialty iPod-accessory Web shops like EverythingiCafe (*http://store.everythingicafe.com*).

DLO's AutoCharger for iPod

Play Games on an iPod

The iPod is a personal entertainment machine on many levels. All iPod Classic and Nano models have three games: iQuiz, Klondike, and Vortex. (These replace the games on older iPods: Brick, Music Quiz, Parachute, and Solitaire.) If you have a modern iPod, you can also buy and download old-school video games like Ms. Pac-Man, Sudoku, and more from the iPod Games area of the iTunes Store (Chapter 7). To find any of your games, go to iPod→Extras→Games.

iQuiz

Complete with colorful flashing graphics and a cheesy, 70's-style game show soundtrack, iQuiz picks your brain with contemporary multiple-choice questions in several trivia categories: music, movies, and TV. The game brings its own questions to the screen, but also taps into your iPod to find out how much you know about your own music library. For people with older video-playing iPods, iQuiz is also for sale in the iTunes Store.

If you get hooked on these trivial pursuits, you can even create your own questions and sync up new quizzes to your iPod. To do so, take a little trip to *www.iquizmaker.com* and download Aspyr Media's free iQuiz Maker software for your Mac or PC.

If you just want to take—instead of make—the quizzes, there's also a Quiz Installer program on the site that lets you load new quizzes made by other people onto your iPod.

You can find more details on becoming an iQuiz master at *www.apple.com/itunes/store/games/iquiz.html*.

Klondike

The old iPod solitaire has been upgraded to an animated, Vegas-style version called Klondike, complete with a clock and your accumulating payout on screen. To play, you get a row of seven card piles, on which you're supposed to alternate black and red cards in descending numerical order.

Use the click wheel to pass the hand over each stack of cards. When you get to the card you want, click the center button to move the selected card to the bottom of the screen. Then scroll the disembodied hand to the pile where you want to place the card, and click the center button again to make the play. Click the face-down card (upper left) for three new cards to choose from.

Maze (Nano only)

The Nano's accelerometer gets a workout in the Maze, a game that has you tilting the iPod around in every direction as you try to work a ball through a series of increasingly complex mazes. You don't have all day to wave the Nano around—you have to make it through the puzzle before the timer runs out.

Vortex

Most computers and handheld devices wouldn't be complete without some brick-bashing version of the old Pong-against-the-wall game. Vortex scales up the basic concept of Brick to 360 degrees of smashing 3-D fun.

Use the scroll wheel to move the bat around the edges of the circular Vortex and audibly smash through the rotating bricks. If you have an older video-playing iPod, Vortex is available for purchase in the games area of the iTunes Store.

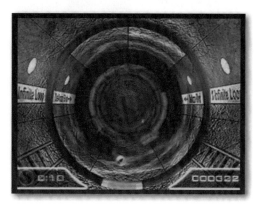

Some Idiot Set the iPod Menus to Greek

Changing the iPod's onscreen language to an unfamiliar alphabet is a favorite trick of jealous co-workers and older brothers. Fortunately, you have a couple of ways to get the iPod back to English.

First, click the Menu button until you get back to the iPod's main menu screen. You'll see "iPod" in English at the top, and the menu listings in whatever language your wisenheimer pal picked out for you. Then follow these steps:

❶ **Scroll down to the sixth line on your iPod.** You've just highlighted the Settings menu; click it.

❷ **Scroll all the way down to "Reset Settings," which conveniently appears in English.** Here, you can make a decision:

Option 1: The *third* menu item from the bottom (that is, the menu item two rows up from "Reset Settings") is the Language setting. Scroll up there to get to the language list and then choose English.

Option 2: If you're tired of your iPod settings, you can wipe them out and start over. Click Reset All Settings. The next screen gives you a choice: Cancel or Reset.

Lock Up Your Pod

When you turn your iPod's Screen Lock feature on, the screen displays a safe's door icon that stubbornly refuses to go away until you enter your combination. To activate this protective layer:

❶ Choose Extras→Screen Lock.

❷ On the next screen, you can pick the numbers for your secret code. Using the click wheel, navigate to each box. By spinning the wheel, pick a number from 0 to 9. Press the center button to enter a number and continue until you fill all four boxes.

❸ Now, when you want to lock your 'Pod, choose Extras→Screen Lock→ Lock. You also have the option to reset your code on this screen.

The iPod displays the Lock screen—even when it's asleep or connected to a computer—until you click the center button and enter the correct combination with the click wheel. If you enter the wrong digits, the lock icon stubbornly refuses to leave the screen.

 This lock's not foolproof: You (or someone else) can always get into the iPod by connecting it to iTunes.

Touring the Touch

Traditional iPods may have their wheels and buttons, but the iPod Touch brings a whole new level of control to your fingertips. In fact, your fingertips are the *way* you control the functions on this very special iPod. Instead of scrolling and clicking through menu after menu, the iPod Touch gives you a set of icons on its Home screen. Tap one and you instantly drop into the place you want to be—whether it's on the Web, amongst your favorite tunes, or in your photo collection.

The Touch comes preloaded with colorful little programs to let you keep tabs on the weather, the stock market, and even your email. But you're not limited to the standard-issue software—thanks to the iTunes App Store, you can turn this iPod into a personalized little pocket computer with its own games, utility programs, ebooks, and more.

This chapter gives you a close-up look at where to find everything on your iPod Touch, and how to customize it to your own personal preferences. And, because playing music on this iPod is truly a hands-on experience, you'll learn everything you need to get your tunes cranked up and responding to your every tap.

Turn iPod Touch On and Off

The iPod Touch has only three physical buttons on the outside. The Sleep/Wake button is the skinny black one on the Touch's top-left edge.

Pressing this tiny sliver of a button once puts the Touch to sleep—that is, into Standby mode. Pressing it again turns on the screen, so it's ready for action.

This small button also works as an On/Off switch for when you want to shut the iPod completely down; just press it down until the screen goes black and a red arrow commanding you to "Slide to power off" appears. Slide your finger across the screen to power down the 'Pod. Press the Sleep/Wake button when you're ready to turn on the Touch again.

The Home Button and Home Screen

The Home button is the one and only *real* button on the front of this iPod. Push it to summon the Home screen, which is your gateway to everything the iPod Touch can do.

Having a Home button is a wonderful thing. It means you can never get lost. No matter how deeply you burrow into the Touch software, no matter how far off track you find yourself, one push of the Home button takes you back to the main screen. Unlike other iPods, with their Menu buttons and retraceable paths through submenus, the Home button is the *only* way out of some screens.

The Home button also wakes up the iPod if it's in Standby mode. That's sometimes easier than finding the Sleep/Wake switch on the top edge.

> **Tip** The Home button is also a "force quit" button. If you press it for six seconds straight, whatever program you're running completely shuts down. That's a good troubleshooting technique when a particular program seems to be acting up.

On the Home screen, you find all your Touchable icons, divided into two distinct groups. On the top part of the screen, you have all your Internet and personal-information applications, including the Safari Web browser, the Mail program, a shortcut to YouTube, a calendar program, an address book, clock, calculator, and the App Store. The Settings icon lets you set your preferences for many of these programs.

Want to rearrange the icons? Press down on an icon until it wiggles, and then drag it to a new location. Press the Home button to make the icons sit still again. Once you fill up the Home screen with icons and applications, swipe your finger to the left to see your next screen full of icons. Swipe that finger the other way to go back to the first screen of icons.

On the bottom part of the Touch is where the fun really begins. Here are the shortcuts to all the music, movies, and photos you copied over from your computer to your iPod. And, thanks to that purple iTunes icon, you're only a wireless network away from getting even more music.

What's in the Music Menu

Tap the Music icon on the iPod Touch and you're instantly transported into a land of lists—lots of lists. The first four icons at the bottom of the screen represent your starter lists, as follows:

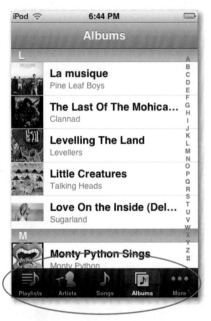

- **Playlists.** A *playlist* is a group of songs that you've placed together, in a sequence that makes sense to you. One might consist of party tunes; another might hold romantic dinner music; a third might be drum-heavy workout cuts. Chapter 6 tells you how to make them.

  Scroll the list by dragging your finger or by flicking. To see what songs are in a playlist, tap its name. (The > symbol in an iPod menu always means, "Tap to see what's in this list.")

- **Artists.** This list identifies all the bands, orchestras, or singers in your collection. Even if you have only one song from a certain performer, it shows up here. Once again, you drill down to the list of individual songs by tapping an artist's name. At that point, tap any song to play it.

- **Songs.** Here's an alphabetical list of every song on your iPod. Scroll or flick through it, or use the index at the right side of the screen to jump to a letter of the alphabet. Tap anything to begin playing it.

- **Albums.** That's right, it's a list of all the CDs from which your music collection is derived, complete with miniature pictures of the album art. Tap an album's name to see a list of songs that came from it.

Those four lists—Playlists, Artists, Songs, Albums—are only suggestions. On an *old-school* iPod, of course, you can slice and dice your music collection in all kinds of other listy ways: by Album, Genre, Composer, and so on.

> **Tip** Here's a universal Touch convention: Anywhere you're asked to *drill down* from one list to another—from a playlist to the songs inside, for example—you can backtrack by tapping the blue button at the upper-left corner of the screen. Its name changes to tell you what screen you came from (Playlists, for example).

You can do that on the iPod Touch, too; there just isn't room across the bottom row to hold more than four list icons at a time.

To view some of the most useful secondary lists, tap the fifth and final icon, labeled More. The More screen appears, listing a bunch of other ways to view your collection:

- **Audiobooks.** One of the great pricey joys of life is listening to digital "books on tape" that you've bought from Audible.com (Chapter 7). They show up in this list. (Audio books you've ripped from CDs don't automatically show up here—only ones you've downloaded from Audible.)

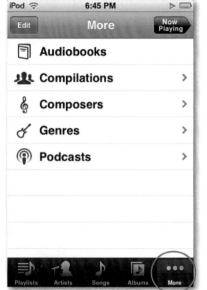

- **Compilations.** A *compilation* is one of those albums that's been put together from many different performers. You know: "Zither Hits of the 1600s," "Kazoo Classics," and so on. You're supposed to turn on the Compilation checkbox manually, in iTunes (in the Preferences box's Advanced tab), to identify songs that belong together in this way. Then, all songs that belong to compilations you've created show up in this list.

- **Composers.** Here's your whole music collection sorted by composer—a crumb the iPod Touch creators have thrown to classical-music fans.

- **Genres.** Tap this item to sort your collection by musical genre (that is, style): Pop, Rock, World, Podcast, Gospel, or whatever.

- **Podcasts.** Here are all your podcasts (Chapter 7), listed by creator. A blue dot indicates that you haven't yet listened to some of the podcasts by a certain podcaster. Similarly, if you tap a podcast's name to drill down, you'll see the individual episodes, once again marked by blue "you haven't heard me yet" dots. (Half a dot means you started listening earlier and stopped, with the remaining time listed under the episode title.)

> **Tip** At the bottom of any of these lists, you'll see the total number of items *in* that list: "76 Songs," for example. At the top of the screen, you may see the Now Playing button, which opens up the playback screen of whatever's playing.

What's in the Videos Menu

Tap this icon for one-stop browsing of all the video material on your iPod Touch, organized by category:

- **Movies.** All your full-length feature films, downloaded movie trailers, and even your own filmmaking efforts live in this menu.

- **TV Shows.** When you're ready to catch up on your TV-watching, check this menu for your iTunes Store-purchased episodes and personally recorded shows.

- **Music Videos.** Music video clips, many of which are now offered as bonus material on iTunes album purchases, hang out here.

- **Video Podcasts.** Podcasts aren't just audio-only these days; look here for the full-blown video productions. (You see only one listing for each podcaster, along with the number of episodes you've got.)

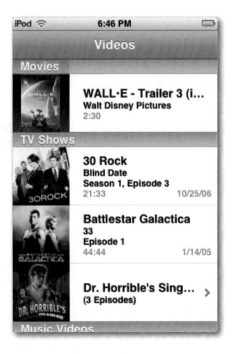

A handy thumbnail photo next to each video gives you a hint as to what's in it, and you also see the total playing time of each one.

You can probably guess, at this point, how you start playing one: by tapping its name. But don't forget to rotate the Touch 90 degrees; all videos play in landscape orientation (the wide way). See Chapter 8 for more on video.

What's in the Photos Menu

The iPod Touch makes an extremely handsome—and portable—pocket photo album and slide carousel. Once you send copies of your favorite digital pictures from your computer to your iPod Touch, they land here in the Photos menu, all within easy reach from the Home screen.

Once you tap Photos, you see all your pictures grouped into one collection known as the Photo Library. If you chose to sync up specific photo albums from Photoshop Elements, iPhoto, or whatever compatible picture program you use, the individual album names are also listed. The gray number in parentheses tells you how many pictures you have in each album.

Tap the name of any album or library to see the pictures. If you want to learn how to set up all this photo fun on your Touch, Chapter 9 has the scoop.

iPod 🔋	9:45 PM	🔋
	Photo Albums	
	Saved Photos (27)	>
	Photo Library (1054)	>
	The Wienermobile! (6)	>
	Hopper & Harrigan (8)	>
	London 2004 (115)	>
	London and Paris... (439)	>
	Gettysburg 2006 (90)	>

> **Tip** See that Saved Photos album at the top of the picture up there? That's where the photos you grab from the Web and email messages are stored on the Touch. To save a photo from a Safari page or a Mail attachment, press your finger on the picture until a Save Image button slides up from the bottom of the screen. Tap the button and your photo is deposited in the Saved Photos album. Any screenshots you take on the Touch (see Chapter 9 for the Tip on that) land in here as well.

What's in the Settings Menu

The iPod Touch is a powerful little media machine, and the Settings menu is where you go to fine-tune the player's preferences to your liking. Here's what you find by tapping the Settings icon on the Home screen:

- **Wi-Fi.** See what network you're connected to (or not), and turn the iPod's Wi-Fi antenna on or off here.

- **Fetch New Data.** If you get your email, contacts, and calendar updates through a "push" service like Microsoft Exchange, Apple's MobileMe, or Yahoo, set your preferences here for how often you get those updates.

- **Brightness.** Sensors can automatically detect the light in the room and adjust the Touch screen brightness, but you can override that here.

- **General.** Here are the settings for the Touch's keyboard, sound effects, screen wallpaper, and auto-lock timer. Controls for network settings and Location Services (the Touch's GPS-like ability to plot your position on a map) are here, too. You'll also find the About screen which tells you how much stuff is on your iPod and its serial number. If you're worried about who can see your iPod's contents, you can assign a four-digit number to unlock the screen in the Passcode settings. In the International area, you can choose the iPod screen's display language or pick an onscreen keyboard designed for typing in French, German, Italian, Japanese, and several other languages. You can also reset all the settings you've been fiddling with in the General area—and even erase all the iPod's content.

- **Music.** Turn the Equalizer and Sound Check features (Chapter 5) off or on, adjust the speed of your audio book narration, and set limits for your maximum volume here.

- **Video.** The Touch can remember where you stopped that video you were watching thanks to a setting here. You can also toggle Closed Captioning on or off. The TV Out settings for pumping the video signal out of the iPod and into a TV are here as well.

- **Photos.** Here's where you set the time for each photo to appear on the screen in a slideshow. You can pick artsy onscreen transitions like "Cube" or "Ripple" between images—and put the whole show on a constant repeat loop (just like TV shows on low-budget cable networks). To keep things interesting, you can also choose to randomly shuffle all the photos during your slideshow.

- **Mail, Contacts, Calendars.** Tap here to set up an email account right on the Touch. You can adjust all other Mail-related preferences here, too (like how often the Touch looks for new messages), and you can delete unwanted accounts. Scroll farther down for the Contacts settings, where you can change the sorting order of the first and last names of people in your iPod Touch's address book. In the Calendars area, you get Time Zone controls for making sure your events are set for your own zone and a toggle to turn new invitation alerts on or off. Chapter 10 has more on syncing contacts and calendars.

- **Safari.** The search and security preferences for the Touch's Wee Wide Web browser are located on this screen. Choose between Yahoo or Google for your default search engine; block pop-up ads and cookies; or clear out all the accumulated Web-page data leftover from your surfing by clearing the cache. Chapter 11 has more on all of this.

- **Nike + Pod.** If you use the Nike + iPod kit in your daily workouts, tap the On button here to place a shortcut on the Touch's Home screen. You can also adjust your preferences for spoken feedback, measuring in miles or kilometers, and your personal "Power Song" to get you motivated.

Other Icons on the Touch Home Screen

The Music, Videos, and Photos icons on the Touch Home screen definitely get a workout, but there are several other icons awaiting your gentle tap as well:

- **Safari.** Take a Web journey, no computer needed. Tap the Safari icon to fire up the browser and check out Chapter 11 to learn how to use it.

- **Calendar.** You can take a copy of your schedule with you from your computer's copy of iCal, Entourage, or Outlook. Chapter 10 tells you how.

- **Mail.** Tap here to check your email—or send some messages.

- **Contacts.** Keep in touch on your Touch with the iPod's address book. See Chapter 10 for the details.

- **YouTube.** Wirelessly snag video clips from one of the world's most popular Web sites. See Chapter 8 for more on YouTube and other iPod video.

- **Stocks.** Check your portfolio and see how the market's doing today. Tap the tiny ❶ in the bottom corner to spin the screen around and add your own ticker symbols to your palm-sized big board.

- **Maps.** Get directions or figure out where you are by tapping the icon in the lower-left corner.

- **Weather.** Current temperatures and forecasts for your favorite cities. Tap ❶ to flip the screen and add new towns. Swipe a finger across the screen to cycle through them.

- **Clock.** You can have one clock in your pocket—or keep time in several cities around the world at once. Chapter 10 shows the way.

- **Calculator.** Tap the Calculator icon to get a big bright math machine, ready to divide and conquer for you. Hold the Touch sideways in its landscape mode to get a scientific calculator for when you need to do trigonometry on the go.

- **Notes.** Tap here to take a memo to yourself using the Touch keyboard.

- **iTunes.** The happy purple icon in the bottom corner is your one-tap trip to music-shopping fun—without wires. Chapter 7 tells you what to expect once you get there.

- **App Store.** You thought that other stuff was fun? Tap here to find games, ebooks, and so much more to tickle your Touch.

Fancier Fingerwork for the iPod Touch

Now that you've mastered the old tap, drag, flick, and slide (see Chapter 1 for a refresher), there are two more iPod Touch moves to add to your repertoire. These maneuvers are used in the player's more visually-oriented programs, like its Safari Web browser, or in Photos and Movies.

Finger Spread and Pinch

Tiny Web page type can be hard to read, or maybe you want to take a more detailed look at a certain photo. To zoom in, place your thumb and index finger on either side of the part you want to see better, and make a spreading motion across the screen to zoom in to that area. To zoom out, pinch your fingers closer together. Chapter 11 is all about using the Web on the Touch, and Chapter 9 shows you how to give your photos (and fingers) a workout.

Double-Tap

You may be used to double-clicking a computer mouse, but on the iPod Touch, one tap usually does it. Still, there are at least two places within the Touch where double-tapping pays off:

- In the Safari Web browser or in Photos, tap the screen twice to quickly zoom in and magnify the area you just tapped.

- When watching a video, tap the screen twice to toggle back and forth between screen aspect ratios—the full-screen view (below, left) where the edges of the frame get cropped off, or widescreen, letterboxed view (right), which movie lovers favor because it's what the director really intended the scene to look like.

Customize Your Touch Menus

The Touch Music menus described earlier in this chapter showed how you can sort your collection by every conceivable criterion. But what if you're a huge podcast nut? Are you really expected to open up the More screen every time you want to see your list of podcasts? Or what if you frequently want access to your audiobooks or composer list?

Fortunately, you can add the icons of these lists to the bottom of the main iPod Touch screen, where the four starter categories now appear (Playlists, Artists, Songs, Albums). That is, you can replace or rearrange the icons that show up here, so that the lists you use most frequently are easier to open.

To renovate the four starter icons, tap the More button and then tap the Edit button (upper-left corner). You arrive at the Configure screen.

Here's the complete list of music-and-video sorting lists: Albums, Podcasts, Audiobooks, Genres, Composers, Compilations, Playlists, Artists, and Songs.

To replace one of the four starter icons at the bottom, use a finger to drag an icon from the top half of the screen downward, directly onto the *existing* icon you want to replace. It lights up to show the success of your drag.

When you release your finger, you'll see that the new icon has replaced the old one. Tap Done in the upper-right corner.

Oh, and while you're there on the Configure screen: You can also take this opportunity to *rearrange* the first four icons at the bottom. Drag them around with your finger. It's fun for the whole family.

Cover Flow in Motion

Anytime you're using the iPod Touch for music, whether you're playing songs or just flipping through your lists, you can rotate the Touch 90 degrees in either direction—so it's in landscape orientation—to turn on Cover Flow. *Nothing* gets oohs and ahhhs from the admiring crowd like Cover Flow.

In Cover Flow, the screen goes dark for a moment—and then it reappears, showing two-inch-tall album covers, floating on a black background. Push or flick with your fingers to make them fly and flip over in 3-D space, as though they're CDs in a record-store rack (remember those?).

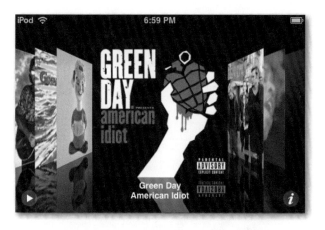

If you tap one (or tap the little ❷ button in the lower-right corner), the album flips around so you can see the "back" of it, containing a list of songs from that album. Tap a song to start playing it; tap the **II** in the lower-left corner to pause. Tap the back (or the ❷ button) again to flip the album cover back to the front and continue browsing.

To turn off Cover Flow, rotate the iPod upright again.

So what, exactly, is Cover Flow for? You could argue that it's a unique way to browse your collection, to seek inspiration in your music without having to stare at scrolling lists of text.

But you could also argue that it's just Apple's engineers showing off.

The Now Playing Screen: The Basics

Whenever a song is playing, the Now Playing screen appears, filled with information and controls for your playback pleasure.

For example:

- **Return arrow.** At the top-left corner of the screen, the fat, left-pointing
  arrow means, "Return to the list whence this song came." It takes you back
  to the list of songs in this album, playlist, or whatever.

- **Song info.** Center top: the artist name, track name, and album name.
  Nothing to tap here, folks. Move along.

Return to list

Songs on
this album

Swipe to
return to list

Volume slider

- **Album list.** At the top-*right* corner, you see a three-line icon that seems
  to say, "list". Tap it to view a list of all songs on *this* song's album.

  On the screen that appears, you're offered three enjoyable activities. You
  can jump directly to another cut by tapping its name. You can check out
  the durations of the songs in this album.

And you can *rate* a song, ranking it from one to five stars, by tapping its name and then tapping one of the five dots at the top of the screen. If you tap dot number 3, for example, then the first three dots all turn into stars. You've just given that song three stars. When you next sync your iPod Touch with your computer, the ratings you've applied magically show up on the same songs in iTunes.

To return to the Now Playing screen, tap the upper-right icon once again. (Once you tap, that icon looks like the album cover.) Or, for a bigger target, double-tap any blank part of the screen.

- **Album art.** Most of the screen is filled with a bright, colorful shot of the original CD's album art. (If none is available—if you're listening to a song *you* wrote, for example—you see a big gray generic musical-note picture.)

Tip You can double-tap the big album art picture to open the track list, too. It's a bigger target.

The Now Playing Screen: Song Maneuvers

Once you're on the Now Playing screen, a few controls await your fingertip—some obvious and some not so obvious.

- **Play/Pause (▶/II) button.** The Pause button looks like this **II** when the music is playing. If you do pause the music, the button turns into the Play button (▶).

- **Previous, Next (I◀◀, ▶▶I).** These buttons work exactly as they do on an iPod. That is, tap I◀◀ to skip to the beginning of this song (or, if you're already at the beginning, to the previous song). Tap ▶▶I to skip to the next song.

If you hold down one of these buttons instead of tapping, you rewind or fast-forward. It's rather cool, actually—you get to hear the music speeding by as you keep your finger down, without turning the singer into a chipmunk. The rewinding or fast-forwarding accelerates if you keep holding down the button.

Tip "Okay," you're saying to yourself, "These playback controls are all well and good when I'm on the Now Playing screen—but what if I'm browsing my photos and I want to skip over this one track I hate? Do I have to tap my way back through the Home screen to Music so I can skip ahead to the next song?"

Not at all. Tap the Home button twice to bring up a mini-control panel where you can get to the playback controls, no matter where you are in the non-Musical parts of the Touch. You can adjust the volume, pause, move to the next or previous track, and even see what's playing. If you need to get back to the Music menu, tap the Music button in the corner to be taken there immediately.

- **Volume.** Drag the round, white handle of this scroll bar (bottom of the screen) to adjust the volume. (You can also use the Volume rocker on the left side of the Touch, if you've got a second-generation model.)

Of course, you probably didn't need a handsome full-color book to tell you what those basic playback controls are for. But there's also a quartet of *secret* controls that don't appear until you tap anywhere on an empty part of the screen (for example, on the album cover):

- **Loop button.** If you *really* love a certain album or playlist, you can command the iPod to play it over and over again, beginning to end. Just tap the Loop button (⟳) so it turns blue (⟳).

- **Scroll slider.** This slider (top of the screen) reveals three useful statistics: how much of the song you've heard, in "minutes:seconds" format (at the left end), how much time remains (at the right end), and which slot this song occupies in the current playlist or album.

  To operate the slider, drag the tiny round handle with your finger. (Just tapping directly on the spot you want to hear doesn't work.)

- **Genius playlist.** Tap the ✳ icon to make a Genius playlist based on this song. Chapter 6 has the details.

- **Shuffle button.** Ordinarily, the iPod plays the songs in an album sequentially, from beginning to end. But if you love surprises, tap the ⤬ button so it turns blue. Now you'll hear the songs on the album in random order.

  To hide the secret buttons, tap an empty part of the screen once again.

  By the way, there's nothing to stop you from turning on *both* Shuffle *and* Loop, meaning that you'll hear the songs on the album played endlessly, but never in the same order twice.

Install (and Uninstall) New Apps

Programs from the App Store give your Touch all sorts of new powers. If you're anxious to try some out, here are two ways to get your Touch tricked out:

- **Buy apps in the iTunes Store.** Click the App Store link on the main Store page. After you've shopped, connect the Touch, and sync 'em up. Chapter 5 explains the fine art of syncing.

- **Buy apps on the Touch.** When you've got a Wi-Fi connection, tap the blue App Store icon on the Home screen and browse away. At the top of the App Store screen, you can tap to see the Top Paid and Top Free programs. At the bottom of the screen, you can find apps grouped under Featured, in Categories, or by the Top 25 apps in the Store. A Search icon (🔍) awaits if you're looking for something specific. When you find an app you want, tap the price icon; it turns into a Buy Now button. Hit that, type in your iTunes Store name and password (even if it's a free application), and the download begins. After the program has finished loading on the Home screen, tap the new icon to launch your new app and start using it.

But it's a fact of life: sometimes apps don't work out. They're not what you thought they'd be, they're buggy and crashy (it happens), or they're taking up too much precious Touch space. Here are two ways to uninstall an app:

- **Remove apps in iTunes.** Connect the Touch to the computer, click its icon in the iTunes window, and click the Applications tab. In the list, deselect the apps you want to remove and then click Sync to uninstall them.

- **Remove apps on the iPod Touch.** On the Home screen, press and hold the unwanted application's icon until an X appears in the wiggling icon's corner. Tap the X, confirm your intention to delete, and wave goodbye to that app. Press the Home button to return to business as usual.

> **Note** See a red circled number on the App Store icon? You've got updates waiting for that number of apps; tap the icon to see what they are. Tap the name of the program you want to update, tap the Price button (don't worry, it's free), and then tap Install. The program upates after you type in your Store password.

Set Up and Check Your Mail

When inside a Wi-Fi hotspot, the Touch is also a traveling email machine that lets you check, write, and send messages. And just as there are two ways to get apps on the Touch, there are also two ways to get your email account settings in place on your mini musical computer.

- **Sync mail settings with iTunes.** You get email on your computer, right? If you're using a dedicated program like Apple Mail or Microsoft Outlook, you can copy those account settings over to the Touch. Connect the Touch to the computer, click its icon in iTunes, and then click the Info tab. Scroll down to Mail Accounts and put a check in the box next to "Sync selected mail accounts." Pick the

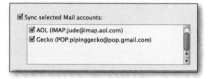

accounts you want to tote around on the Touch. Click Sync or Apply to copy the settings—but not your computer-based messages—over to the Touch, where you can check mail on the run.

- **Set up mail accounts on the Touch.** Tap the Mail icon. If you use Exchange, MobileMe, Gmail, Yahoo, or AOL, tap the appropriate icon. If you don't use any of those, tap Other. On the next screen, type in your name, email address, password, and a short description ("Personal Gmail", say). If you tapped Other, be prepared to type in the same settings you got from your Internet provider when you signed up for the account. Click Save and the

Mail program goes out and gets your new messages. Need help sorting through email geekery like the difference between IMAP and POP? Check out this book's "Missing CD" page at *www.missingmanuals.com*.

Mail on the Touch looks and works pretty much like any other email program. Here's the layout:

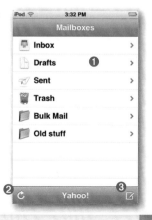

❶ **Mailboxes.** Your incoming, outgoing, and drafts (saved messages-in-progress) live here.

❷ **Check for new mail.** Tap the circular arrow to see if you have fresh messages.

❸ **Write a new message.** Tap the icon in the bottom-right corner to fire up a new message. Fill in the address, your thoughts, and tap Send.

4

File Edit View Controls Store Advanced Help
iTunes
Fireworks
Schoolhouse Rocks The Vote
0:12
-2:26
View
Search
LIBRARY
Music
Movies
TV Shows
Podcasts
Audiobooks
Applications
Radio
Ringtones
STORE
iTunes Store
Selected Item
Genre
All (19 Genres)
Alternative & Punk
Blues
Classical
Country
Easy Listening
Electronica/Dance
Folk
Gospel & Religious
Artist
All (54 Artists)
Compilations
Antony & The Johnsons
Bear McCreary
Beyoncé
Billy Bragg & Wilco
The Blind Boys of Alabama
Bryan Ferry & Roxy Music
David Frizzell & Shelly West
Album
All (76 Albums)
Antony & The Johnsons
Any Which Way You Can
Appalachian Journey
Battlestar Galactica: Season
Beethoven - Symphony No.
Best Of Isley Brothers
Name
Album
Artist
Time
Rock The Vote
I'm Just A Bill
Sufferin' 'Till Suffrage
The Campaign Trail
The Preamble
Do You Wanna Party
Fireworks
Three-Ring Government
Get To Know Your Electora...
Messin' With My Bill Of Rights
Schoolhouse Rock...
The Virtuals
Joan Osborne, Issa...
Etta James
Bob Dorough
John Popper
Essra Mohawk & Th...
The Sugarhill Gang
The Roots with Jazz...
Spicy T & Shihan
Grady Tate
3:47
3:02
3:54
2:34
2:39
3:03
2:39
3:56
3:03
2:48
Genius Sidebar
The Sugarhill Gang
Top Albums
Rapper's Delight ...
The Sugarhill Gang
$0.99
BUY
The Essentials: ...
The Sugarhill Gang
$9.90
BUY
Top Songs You're Missing
Rapper's Delight
The Sugarhill Gang
$0.99
Apache
The Sugarhill Gang
$0.99
8th Wonder
The Sugarhill Gang
$0.99
Rapper's Reprise
The Sugarhill Gang
$0.99
Sugarhill Groove
The Sugarhill Gang
$0.99
809 songs, 2 days, 2.86 GB

iTunes Basics

If you read Chapter 1 for a speedy way to get your iPod set up and ready to play, you've already dipped a toe in the iTunes waters. But as you may have guessed, beneath its pretty surface, iTunes is a deep well of media-management wonders.

Even without buying music from the online iTunes Store, you can use the program to import music from your CD collection and add personal ratings, lyrics, and artwork to your song files. Once you check everything into your iTunes library, the program makes it easy to browse and search through all your treasures—and automatically mix your music.

Yes, iTunes is a powerful program. So powerful, in fact, that this chapter is mainly going to focus on introducing you to its most basic and useful functions—like what the controls do and how to import music from CDs. If you want to learn more about fine-tuning your library, Chapter 5 covers more advanced iTunes features. Chapter 6 tells you how to create customized song playlists, Chapter 7 is all about blowing your bucks in the iTunes Store, and Chapter 8 spotlights the video side of iTunes.

But enough of the introductory blah-blah. Turn the page if you want to get to know iTunes better.

The iTunes Window: An Introduction

iTunes is your iPod's best friend. You can do just about everything with your digital music here, from converting songs on a CD into iPod-ready music files, buying music, listening to Internet radio stations, watching video—and more.

Here's a quick tour of the main iTunes window and what all the buttons, controls, and sliders do.

The Source panel on the left side of iTunes displays all the audio and video you can tap into at the moment. Click any item listed in the Source column to display its contents in the main window, like so:

❶ Click any icon in the Library group to see what's in your different media libraries. As you add movies, music, and other stuff to iTunes, click the appropriate icon to find the type of thing—a song, a TV show—you're looking for. Programs you buy for the iPod Touch land here under Applications.

❷ In the Store area, click the icons to shop for new stuff in the iTunes Store or see the list of things you've already purchased. There's also a Downloads list for items you're downloading from the Store, or files that are ready for you to snag.

❸ If a music CD is in your computer's drive it shows up in the Devices area, as will a connected iPod. Click the gray Eject icon next to the name to safely disconnect an iPod or pop out a disc.

❹ In the Shared area, browse the music libraries of other iTunes fans on your network and play their music on your own computer.

❺ The Playlists section is where iTunes keeps all your custom song lists. The Party Shuffle feature, which lets you play DJ, lives here too.

❻ When you click an area of the Source list, iTunes' main window displays all the things in that category—Music, in this case. Above the main song list are three columns that let you browse through the genres, artists, and albums in your collection. Naturally, this part of the window is called the Browser.

The outer edges of the iTunes window are full of buttons and controls:

❼ Play and pause your current song or video— or jump to the next or previous track. The volume slider adjusts the sound.

❽ The center of the upper pane shows you what song's playing. To the right of that you have handy buttons to change views within the main part of the window and a search box for finding songs fast.

❾ At the bottom-left corner are short-cut buttons for (from left to right) making a new playlist, shuffling or repeating your playlists, and display-ing album artwork or videos.

❿ The lower-right corner of iTunes is where the Genius controls hang out. When you have a song selected, click the whizzy electron-shaped icon to make a Genius playlist (Chapter 6) based on that song. The boxed-arrow icon toggles the Genius Sidebar panel on (it's stocked with "Buy these songs" suggestions to help round out your library), and off (to leave you in peace).

Change the Look of the iTunes Window

Don't be misled by the brushed-aluminum look of iTunes: You can push and pull various window parts like salt-water taffy.

- Adjust the height of the iTunes Browser—the three-pane wide quick-browse area that opens and closes when you press Ctrl+B/⌘-B on the keyboard—by dragging the tiny dot at the bottom of the Browser up or down.

- The main song list is separated into columns, which you can sort or re-arrange. Click a column title (like Name or Artist) to sort the list alphabeti-cally. Click the column title again to reverse the sorting order. Change the order of the columns by dragging them, as shown above.

- To adjust a column's width, drag the right-hand vertical divider line. (You may need to grab the line in the column title bar.)

- To resize all columns so their contents fit precisely, right-click (Control-click) any column title and choose Auto Size All Columns.

- To add (or delete) columns, right-click (Control-click) any column title. From the pop-up list of column categories (Bit Rate, Date Added, and so on), choose the column name you want to add or remove. Checkmarks indicate currently visible columns.

- Click the black triangle in the first column to dis-play or hide album covers alongside the song titles. If you don't have any artwork for the song, iTunes displays the generic Gray Musical Note icon. If you find life has too many gray areas already, the next chapter tells you how to add album artwork to your files.

Change the Size of the iTunes Window

Lovely as iTunes is, it takes up a heck of a lot of screen real estate. When you're working on other things, you can shrink it down. In fact, iTunes can run in three size modes: small, medium, or large:

 Large. What you get the first time you open iTunes. (Hate the music hard-sell from the Genius Sidebar on the right side of the window? Close the panel by clicking the square button in the lower-right corner.)

 *Medium.* Windows folks: Switch back and forth between large and medium by pressing Ctrl+M or choosing Advanced→"Switch to Mini Player". If you use iTunes on a Mac, click the green zoom button at the top-left corner (or choose Window→Zoom).

❸ *Small.* To really scrunch things down, start with the medium-size window. Then drag the resize handle (the diagonal lines in the lower-right corner) leftward. To expand it, just reverse the process.

Tired of losing your mini-iTunes window among the vast stack of open windows on your screen? You can make it so that the iTunes mini-player is *always* visible on top of other open documents, windows, and other screen detritus. Just open iTunes Preferences (Ctrl+comma/⌘-comma), click the Advanced tab, and turn on the checkbox next to "Keep Mini Player on top of all other windows." Now you won't have to click frantically trying to find iTunes if you get caught listening to your bubblegum-pop playlist when you thought nobody was around.

Import Specific Songs From Your CDs

In Chapter 1 you learned how iTunes simplifies converting (also called *ripping*) songs from your compact discs into small iPod-ready digital files: You basically just pop a CD into your computer's disc drive and iTunes walks you through the process. If you're connected to the Internet, iTunes downloads song titles and other album info. A few minutes later, you've got copies of those tunes in iTunes.

If you want time to think about *which* songs you want from each CD, no problem. Simply summon the Preferences box (Ctrl+comma/⌘-comma), click the General tab, and then change the menu next to "When you insert a CD:" to "Show CD."

> **Tip** If you know you want all the songs on that stack of CDs next to your computer, just change the iTunes CD import preferences to "Import CD and Eject" to save yourself some clicking.

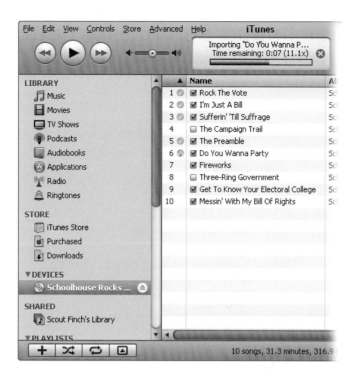

So now, if you don't want the entire album—who wants anything from Don McLean's *American Pie* besides the title track?—you can exclude the songs you *don't* want by removing the checkmarks next to their names. Once you've picked your songs, in the bottom-right corner of the screen, click the Import CD button.

You can Ctrl+click (⌘-click) any box to deselect all checkboxes at once. To do the reverse, Ctrl+click (⌘-click) a box next to an unchecked song to turn them all on again. This is a great technique when you want only one or two songs in the list; turn *all* checkboxes off, and then turn those *two* back on again.

As the import process starts, iTunes moves down the list of checked songs, converting each one to a file in your My Documents→My Music→iTunes→iTunes Music folder (Home→Music→iTunes→iTunes Music). An orange squiggle next to a song name means the track is currently converting. Feel free to switch to other programs, answer email, surf the Web, and do other work while the ripping is under way.

Once the process is done, each imported song bears a green checkmark, and iTunes signals its success with a little melodious flourish. Now you have some brand-new songs in your iTunes music library.

Change Import Settings for Better Audio Quality

The iPod can play several different digital audio formats: AAC, MP3, WAV, AIFF, and a newer format called Apple Lossless. Feel free to safely ignore that last sentence, as well as the rest of this page, if you're *happy* with the way your music sounds on the iPod or a pair of external speakers.

If you find the audio quality lacking, you need to change the way iTunes encodes, or *converts*, those tracks during the CD conversion process. iTunes gives you two main options in its import settings box (Edit [iTunes]→Preferences→General. Click the Import Settings button to get there):

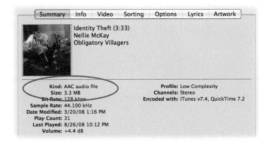

- **Format (pull-down menu: "Import Using").** Some formats tightly compress audio data to save space. The tradeoff: lost sound quality. Highly compressed formats include AAC (iTunes' default setting) and MP3. Formats that use little or no compression include WAV and AIFF, which sound better, but take up more space. Apple Lossless splits the difference: Better sound quality than AAC and MP3, but not as hefty as WAV or AIFF.

- **Bit rate ("Setting").** The higher the number of bits listed, the greater the amount of data contained in the file (in other words, your files take up more storage space). The advantage? Better sound quality.

To see a song's format and other technical informa-tion, click its title in iTunes, press Ctrl+I (⌘-I), and then click the Summary tab in the Get Info box.

Three Ways to Browse Your Collection

Instead of just presenting you with boring lists of songs and albums, iTunes gives you three options for browsing your media collection—some of them more visual than others. Click the View button at the top of iTunes to switch between views.

- **List** presents the traditional way of seeing your song titles. Press Ctrl+B (⌘-B) on the keyboard to toggle on and off the Browser part of the window that shows a pane grouping your music by Artist, Album, and Genre. Press Ctrl+Alt+3 (Option-⌘-3) to jump back to List from another view.

- **Grid View** presents your collection in a nifty array of album covers and other artwork. This grid can be sorted by Album, Artist, Genre, and Composer. There's a lot to do with Grid View, so flip the page for more. Press Ctrl+Alt+4 (Option-⌘-4) to switch to the Grid.

- **Cover Flow.** If you *really* like album art, this view's for you. Ctrl+Alt+5 (Option-⌘-5) is the shortcut. In the top part of iTunes, your collection appears as a stream of album covers. To browse, press the left and right arrow keys on the keyboard or drag the scroll bar underneath the albums to see them whiz by. Click the little Full Screen button by the slider bar to turn your whole screen into Cover View, complete with playback controls.

Get a Birds-Eye Look at Your Collection with Grid View

Grid View is probably the most eye-catching new feature of iTunes 8. It's like laying out all your albums on the living room floor—great for seeing everything you've got, without the hassle of having to pick it all back up. More picturesque than List view and not quite as moving as Cover Flow, Grid View is the middle road to discovering (or rediscovering) what's in your iTunes library.

iTunes offers four different ways to see your collection: grouped by Album, Artist, Genre, or Composer. Click each named tab to see the music sorted by that category. Here's how to work the Grid:

- Hover the mouse over any tile on the grid to get a clickable Play icon that lets you start listening to the music right there.

- Double-click a cover in Album view to display both the cover and song titles in List view.

- If you have mutliple albums under the Artists, Genre, or Composer tabs, hover the mouse across each tile to see the different album covers.

- Adjust the size of the covers and art by dragging the slider at the top of the window.

One thing about Grid View, though: It's pretty darn depressing unless you have artwork on just about everything in your collection. (If you don't and see far too many generic musical-note icons in there, Chapter 5 shows you how to art things up.) And if you hate Grid View, don't use it—iTunes just defaults to whatever view you were using the last time you quit the program.

Search for Songs in iTunes

You can call up a list of all the songs with a specific word in their title, album name, or artist attribution, just by clicking the Source pane's Music icon (under Library) and typing a few letters into the Search box in iTunes' upper-right corner. With each letter you type, iTunes shortens the list of songs that are visible, displaying only tracks that match what you've typed.

For example, typing *train* brings up a list of everything in your music collection that has the word "train" somewhere in the song's information—maybe the song's title ("Mystery Train"), the band name (Wire Train), or the Steve Earle album (*Train A Comin'*). Click the other Library icons like Movies or Audiobooks to search those collections for titles that match your search terms.

Another way to search for specific titles is to use the iTunes Browser mentioned earlier in this chapter. If the Browser pane isn't showing on screen, press Ctrl+B (⌘-B) to summon it. The Browser reveals your collection grouped by Artist, Album, and Genre. Hit those keys again to close the Browser.

Tip If you find List view deadly dull without art, a quick keyboard shortcut pops open the Artwork column next to the song titles from that album. Just press Ctrl+G (⌘-G) to jazz up the List window with graphics. After all, Grid View and Cover Flow can't have all the visual fun now, can they?

Shuffle Your Music in Many Ways

With its sometimes uncanny ability to randomly pluck and play songs that just seem perfect together, the Shuffle feature has won over a huge number of fans, especially those who don't want to think about what to listen to as they noodle around the Internet. To start shuffling just click the twisty arrows icon down on the bottom-left corner of the iTunes window.

You're not stuck with a single shuffling method, either. Some days you may feel like mixing up your music song by song, and other days you may be more in a mood to change things up by album.

You can control just what you shuffle by choosing Controls→Shuffle and selecting Songs, Albums, or Groupings from the submenu. (As explained in the next chapter, Grouping is a way to keep cetain tracks together in your iTunes library, like separate movements that are part of a larger work in the Classical music category.)

Animate Your Songs: iTunes Visualizer

Visualizer is the iTunes term for an onscreen laser-light show that pulses, beats, and dances in perfect sync to your music. The effect is hypnotic and wild, especially when summoned midway through a sluggish day in the office.

With iTunes 8, there are more visuals than ever to pick from. Choose View→Visualizer to select from *iTunes Visualizer* (lots of Disco in Space moments) or *iTunes Classic Visualizer* (trippy psychedelic patterns a go-go). Mac users running OS X 10.5, or later, even get three more colorful themes to choose from: *Lathe*, *Jelly*, and *Stix*.

❶ To summon the scenery, choose View→Show Visualizer. The show begins immediately.

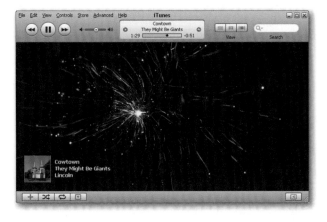

> **Tip** The keyboard shortcut for turning the Visualizer off and on is Ctrl+T (⌘-T).

❷ If you find the iTunes window too constraining for all this eye candy, you can play it full screen by going to the Preferences box (Ctrl+comma/⌘-comma) and clicking the Advanced tab. Put a check in the box next to "Display visualizer full screen."

True, you won't get a lot of work done, but when it comes to stress relief, visuals are a lot cheaper than a hot tub.

5

iTunes Power Moves

Now that you've seen how easy iTunes makes converting your favorite CD tracks into small, great-sounding files, it's time to get down to some serious listening and tune-tweaking. Here, you can do things like assign star ratings to songs and albums, share music with other folks on your network, and even add album artwork to your tracks.

You'll also learn how to use iTunes as editor: the program gives you the tools to even out wildly jarring song volumes, edit out boring on-stage banter on live recordings, and apply preset or custom equalizer settings to tracks. And once you get everything tuned up to your liking, you'll learn how to add, delete, and manually manage the music on your iPod.

Finally, you'll learn how iTunes can help with a vital—but often ignored—part of music management: backing it all up for safe-keeping in case your hard drive croaks and takes all your songs with it.

You're the Critic: Rate Your Music

Although there's no way to give a song two thumbs up within iTunes, you can assign an album or each song in your collection a star rating (one to five). Then you can use your personal ratings to easily produce nothing but playlists of the greatest hits on your hard drive.

If you assign an entire album a single rating, *all* songs on that album get the same number of stars. If you decide to rate individual tracks but not the whole album, the album rating shows the average number of stars per song—so those albums with two good songs and a bunch of filler show an overall mediocre album rating.

❶ To add ratings, first make sure the Album Rating and/or Rating columns are turned on in the iTunes View Options box (Ctrl+J [⌘-J]).

❷ In the Ratings columns (in the iTunes main window), drag the mouse across the column to create one to five stars.

❸ Once you've assigned ratings, you can sort your list by star rating (click the Album Rating or Rating column title), create a Smart Playlist of only your personal favorites (File→New Smart Playlist; choose Album Rating or Rating from the first drop-down menu), and so on.

You can even rate songs on the iPod and your ratings will transfer back to iTunes when you sync up. To rate a song on the iPod, start playing it and tap the Select button a few times until you see dots on screen. Use the scroll wheel to transform the dots into the number of stars you feel the song deserves. Your star ratings also show up on the iPod's Now Playing screen.

Tip If you're more menu-oriented, you can see stars from up top in the iTunes menus. With a track selected, choose File→Rating, slide over to the submenu, and apply the number of stars you feel the song deserves. This is also the place to go if you've inadvertently rated a song: Choose None to return a song to its pristine, unrated condition.

Listen to Internet Radio

Not satisfied with being a mere virtual jukebox, iTunes also serves as an international radio—without the shortwave static. You can find everything from mystical Celtic melodies to Zambian hip hop.

Computers with high-speed Internet connections have a smoother streaming experience, but the vast and eclectic mix of music is well worth checking out—even with a dial-up modem. Just click the Radio icon in the Source list to see a list of stations.

If you find your radio streams are constantly stuttering and stopping, summon the Preferences box (Ctrl+comma/⌘-comma). Click the Advanced icon or tab on the right side of the box. Then, from the Streaming Buffer Size pop-up menu, choose Large. Click OK.

Having the buffer set to Large may increase the waiting time before the music starts playing, but it allows iTunes to hoard more music at once to help make up for interruptions caused by network traffic.

Once you've listened to all the stations listed in iTunes, hit the Internet. You can find more radio stations at sites like *www.shoutcast.com* and you can play them through iTunes when you click the link to listen. (You may need to double-click an automatically downloaded *.pls* file—that's the iTunes playlist extension—in order to start the broadcast.)

Share Your Music

Now that you've built a fabulous music collection, you may feel like sharing it. You can, under one condition: Your fellow sharers are on the same part of your computer network. For instance, any family member on your home network: kosher. Cousin Ferdinand, living in another state: not kosher.

To "publish" your tunes to the network, call up the Preferences box (Ctrl+comma/⌘-comma) and then click the Sharing tab. Turn on "Share my library on my local network." You can choose to share your entire collection or just selected playlists. (You can also tell your own computer to look for other people's Shared music here, too.)

You can also require a password to your own music library—a handy feature if you feel folks mooch off of you quite enough. Finally, click the General tab in this same preferences box. Whatever you type in the Library Name box will show up in your friend's iTunes Source list.

It's easy to listen to somebody else's music; once it's been shared, their iTunes libraries appear right in your Source list. Double-click the desired song to fire it up and play through your computer's speakers. (If your pal has put a password on the collection, you'll have to type that in before you can listen.)

Change a Song's File Format

Sometimes you've got a song already in iTunes whose format you want to change—maybe you need to convert an AIFF file before loading it onto your iPod Shuffle. First, head over to Edit→Preferences (iTunes→Preferences), click the General tab and then the Import Settings button. From the Import Using pop-up menu, pick the format you want to convert *to* and then click OK.

Now, in your iTunes library, select the song you want to convert and then choose Advanced→Create MP3 Version (or AAC, AIFF, or whatever format you just picked).

If you have a whole folder or disk full of potential converts, hold down the Shift (Option) key as you choose Advanced→"Convert to AAC" (or your chosen encoding format). A window pops up, which you can use to navigate to the folder or disk holding the files you want to convert. The only files that don't get converted are protected ones: Audible.com tracks and AAC songs purchased from the iTunes Store.

The song or songs in the original format, as well as the freshly converted tracks, are now in your library.

Even Out Your Songs' Volume Level

No longer must you strain to hear delicate Chopin piano compositions on one track, only to suffer from melted eardrums when Slayer kicks in on the next track. The Sound Check feature attempts to even out disparate volumes, making softer songs louder and gently lowering the real screamers in your library. Audiophiles may nitpick about the Sound Check function, but it can be quite useful, especially for times—like bicycling uphill—when constantly grabbing at the iPod's volume controls is inconvenient.

The first step to using Sound Check is to turn it on. In iTunes, open the Preferences box (Ctrl+comma/⌘-comma). Click the Playback icon or tab and turn on the box for Sound Check.

You also need to turn on Sound Check on the iPod itself: On the Nano, go to the iPod's main screen, choose Settings→Playback→Sound Check and click the Select button. On the Classic, choose Settings→Sound Check. On the iPod Touch choose Settings→Music and then tap Sound Check "On". The next time you connect the iPod to your computer, iTunes will make the necessary audio adjustments to protect your ears.

> **Tip** In that same Playback Preferences box, you can fiddle with the Sound Enhancer slider, which is supposed to add "depth" to your music (try it to see if it does) and overlap the beginnings and endings of your songs, DJ-style with the Crossfade Playback slider.

Set Up Multiple iTunes Libraries

Many households have just one computer for the whole family. If everyone's using the same copy of iTunes, you soon get the Wiggles bumping up against Wu-Tang Clan when you have iTunes shuffling all the tracks, or when you're autosyncing multiple iPods. Wouldn't it be great if everyone had a *personal* iTunes library to have and to hold, to sync and to shuffle, all those different musical tastes—separately? Absolutely.

To use multiple iTunes libraries, just follow these steps:

❶ **Quit iTunes.**

❷ **Hold down the Shift [Option] key on your PC or Mac keyboard and launch iTunes.** In the box that pops up, click Create Library. Give it a name, like "Tiffany's Music" or "Songs My Wife Hates."

❸ **iTunes opens up, but with a blank library with nothing in it.** If you have a bunch of music in your main library that you want to move over to this one, choose File→"Add to Library".

❹ **Navigate to the music you want and add it.** If the songs are in your original library, they're probably in My Documents→My Music→iTunes→iTunes Music [Home→Music→iTunes→iTunes Music] in folders sorted by Artist name. Choose the files you want to add.

To switch between libraries, just hold down the Shift [Option] key when you're starting iTunes, and you'll get a box that lets you pick the one you want. (The program opens the last library used if you don't choose one.) Tracks from CDs you rip go into whatever library's open. And now that you have those songs in this library, you can switch back to the other one and get rid of them there.

Improve Your Tunes with the Graphic Equalizer

If you'd like to improve the way your songs sound, use iTunes' graphic equalizer (EQ) to adjust various frequencies in certain types of music—say, higher bass tones to emphasize the booming rhythm for dance tracks.

To get the Equalizer front and center, choose View (Window)→Show Equalizer and unleash some of your new EQ powers.

❶ Drag the sliders (bass on the left, treble on the right) to accommodate the strengths and weaknesses of your speakers or headphones (and listening tastes). You can drag the Preamp slider up or down to help compensate for songs that sound too loud or soft. To design your own custom preset pattern, click the pop-up menu and select Make Preset.

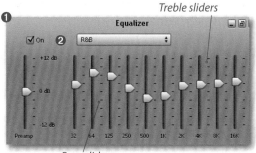

Treble sliders

Bass sliders

❷ Use the pop-up menu to choose one of the canned presets designed for Classical, Dance, Jazz, and so on.

You can apply the same equalizer setting to an entire album or you can select different settings for individual songs.

❸ To apply settings to a whole album, select the album's name (either in Grid View or in the iTunes browser pane). Then press Ctrl+I (⌘-I) and click "Yes" if iTunes asks whether you're sure you want to edit multiple items. In the box that pops up, click the Options tab and choose your preferred setting from the Equalizer Preset pull-down menu.

Note *Equalization* is the art of adjusting the frequency response of an audio signal. An equalizer emphasizes or boosts some of its frequencies while lowering others. In the range of audible sound, *bass* frequency is the low rumbly noise; *treble* is at the opposite end with the high, even shrill sound; and *midrange* is, of course, in the middle, and it's the most audible to human ears.

❹ You can apply these equalizer presets to specific songs as well. Instead of selecting the album name, click the song name in the iTunes window, and then press Ctrl+I (⌘+I). Click the Options tab and choose a setting from the Equalizer Preset menu.

❺ Finally, you can make an Equalizer pop-up tab appear as one of the iTunes columns. Choose Edit→View Options and turn on the Equalizer checkbox. A new column appears right in iTunes from which you can change your EQ settings.

Tip The iPod itself has more than 20 equalizer presets you can use on the go. To set your iPod's Equalizer to a setting designed for a specific type of music, on the Nano choose iPod→Playback→Settings→EQ. (On the Classic, it's iPod→Settings→EQ.) Scroll down the list of presets until you find one that matches your music style, and then press the Select button. The preset's name is now listed next to EQ on the Settings menu. The process works pretty much the same way on the iPod Touch, except you can find the EQ choices at Settings→Music→EQ.

Find (and Get Rid of) Duplicate Songs

Accidentally pulled more than one copy of *Yesterday* into iTunes and find yourself lamenting the wasted megabytes of precious hard drive space? Put iTunes on Double Duty—you can have the program seek out and round up duplicate songs. Just click the Library icon or a playlist icon in the iTunes Source list, and then choose File→Show Duplicates.

Name	Artist	Album by Year	Trac
☑ Feelin' Good	Little Junior's Blue Flames	Sun Records - 25 Blues Classics	
☑ Feelin' Good	Little Junior's Blue Flames	Sun Records : 25 All-Time Greatest H...	
☑ Get Back	The Beatles	Let It Be... Naked	
☑ Get Back	The Beatles	1967-1970	
☑ Hallelujah	k.d. lang	Hymns of the 49th Parallel	
☑ Hallelujah	k.d. lang	Hymns of the 49th Parallel	
☑ Hello, Goodbye	The Beatles	Anthology 2 (Disc 2)	
☑ Hello, Goodbye	The Beatles	1967-1970	
☑ Hey Ya!	Outkast	Speakerboxxx/The Love Below (Andr...	
☑ Hey Ya!	Outkast	Speakerboxxx/The Love Below (Andr...	
☑ Honey	Moby	Holes Soundtrack	
☑ Honey	Moby	Play	

Displaying Duplicates
Show All

96 items, 4.8 hours, 320.7 MB

After iTunes locates all the dupes, it shows them in its main window with a notice at the bottom that reads, "Displaying Duplicates." Here, you can look through and delete extra copies you don't need. But before you start whacking away, make sure these are *true* duplicates—and not two versions of the same tune by different people, two separate performances (like a live and a studio version), or a version of the same song from its original album and one from a soundtrack compilation.

Once you've cleaned up your library, at the bottom of the iTunes window, click Show All to clear out the list of duplicates and show your full collection in all its glory.

Change a Song's Start and Stop Times

Got a song with a bunch of onstage chitchat before it starts or after the music ends? Fortunately, you don't have to sit there and listen. You can change a song's start and stop times so you hear only the juicy middle part.

As you play the song you want to adjust, observe the iTunes status display window; watch for the point in the timeline where you get bored. Then:

❶ Click the track you want to adjust.

❷ Choose File→Get Info (Ctrl+I [⌘-I]) to call up the song's information box.

❸ Click the Options tab and take a look at the Stop Time box, which shows the full duration of the song.

❹ Enter the new stopping point for the song, as you noted earlier.

You can perform the exact same trick at the beginning of a song by adjusting the time value in the Start Time box. The shortened version plays in iTunes and on the iPod, but the additional recorded material isn't really lost. If you ever change your mind, go back to the song's Options box and return the song to its full length.

Edit Song Information

Tired of seeing so many tunes named *Untitled*? You have a couple of different ways to change song titles in iTunes—for example, to enter a song's real name or to fix a typo.

In the song list, click the text you want to change, wait a moment, and then click again. The title now appears highlighted and you can edit the text—just like when you change a file name on the desktop.

Another way to change the song's title, artist name, or other information is to click the song in the iTunes window and press Ctrl+I (⌘-I) to summon the Get Info box. (Choose File→Get Info if you forget the keyboard shortcut.) Click the Info tab and type in the new track information.

Tip Once you've got a song's Get Info box on screen, use the Previous and Next buttons to navigate to other tracks grouped with it in the iTunes song list window. This way, if you want to rapidly edit all track information on the same playlist, on the same album, and so on, you don't have to keep closing and opening each song's box.

Edit Album Information

You don't have to adjust your track information on a song-by-song basis. You can edit an entire album's tracks simultaneously by clicking the Album name in the iTunes browser (or on its cover in Grid View) and pressing Ctrl+I (⌘-I) to bring up the Get Info box.

Ever careful, iTunes flashes an alert box asking if you really want to change the info for a bunch of things all at once. Click Yes.

You can make all sorts of changes to an album in the four-tabbed box that pops up. Here are just a few examples:

❶ Fix a typo or mistake in the Album or Artist name boxes.

❷ Manually add an album cover or photo of your choice to the whole album by dragging it into the Artwork box.

❸ Click the Options tab and change the Equalizer preset for all the songs.

❹ Have iTunes skip the album when you're shuffling music—great for keeping winter holiday music out of your summer barbecue album rotation.

❺ Tell iTunes to play back the album without those two-second gaps between tracks by choosing the "Gapless album" option. (Perfect for opera and *Abbey Road*!)

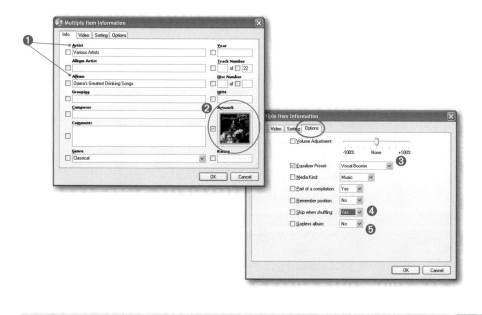

Fetch Missing Album Covers

Songs you download from the iTunes Store often include artwork—usually a picture of the album cover. iTunes displays the picture in the lower-left corner of its main window (you may need to click the Show Artwork icon at lower left). Covers also appear in both the Grid and Cover Flow views. But even if you ripped most of your music from your own CDs, you're not stuck with art-less tracks. You can ask iTunes to head to the Internet and try to find as many album covers for your music as it can.

You need a (free) iTunes Store account to make this work, so if you haven't signed up yet, flip ahead to Chapter 7 to learn how. To make iTunes go fetch, choose Advanced→Get Album Artwork. Since Apple has to root around in your library to figure out what covers you need, you get an alert box warning you that the company will be getting personal information from you (but it's not laughing at your Bay City Rollers tracks).

Then go fetch yourself a sandwich while iTunes gets to work. If you have a huge library, this may take a little while. When iTunes finishes, though, you should have a healthy dose of album art whizzing by in Cover Flow view or filling up the Grid in the middle of the iTunes window.

If iTunes can't find certain album covers on its own, it gives you a message with a list of the artwork it couldn't track down. You can use this helpful list to hunt for and place the art yourself, as described next...

Replace Album Covers Manually

Despite its best intentions, sometimes iTunes can't find an album cover (or retrieves the wrong one). If that happens, take matters into your own hands by manually adding your own album artwork—or even the photo of your choice instead. If Pachelbel's *Canon in D* makes you think of puppies, you can have baby dachshund photos appear in iTunes every time you play that song.

❶ To add your own art to a song, pick a photo or image—JPEG files are the most common.

❷ If you found the cover on Amazon (*hint*: a great source!), save a copy of the image by dragging it off the Web page to your desktop or right-clicking and choosing the "Save Image" option in your Web browser.

❸ With your image near the iTunes window, select the song and click the Show Artwork button in the bottom-left corner of the iTunes window.

❹ Drag the image into the iTunes Artwork pane to add it to the song file.

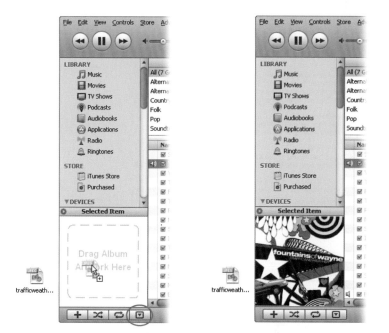

Tip You can also click a song title, type Ctrl+I (⌘-I) to bring up the Get Info box, and then click the Artwork tab. Then just click the Add button to call up a navigation box that lets you choose an image from your hard drive.

Find and Add Lyrics to Your Song Files

You can store a song's lyrics inside the song file just as you do with album art. To add lyrics to a song, select it in iTunes and press Ctrl+I (⌘-I) to call up the song's Get Info box. Then click the Lyrics tab.

Here, you can either meticulously type in a song's verses or look them up on one of the hundreds of Web sites devoted to cataloging lyrics. Once you find your words, getting them into iTunes is merely a cut 'n' paste job away. If you want to add lyrics to all the songs on an album, or have several to do on the same playlist, click the Next button (circled). That advances you to the next song, thereby saving yourself repeated keystrokes invoking the Get Info command.

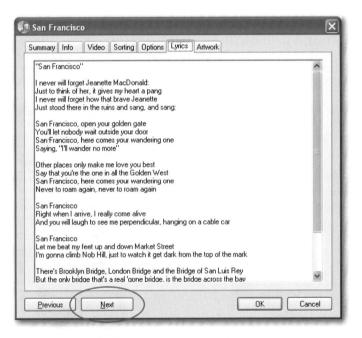

Tip Some types of iTunes files don't support the lyrics function. AAC and MP3 are perfectly happy with lyrics, but QuickTime and WAV files can't handle words, so you need to convert that WAV of "Jumping Jack Flash" if you want to have a gas, gas, gas with lyrics. If your Nano is set to shake and shuffle (page 36), you don't see this option.

View Lyrics on the iPod

Now that you've spent all this time grooming your song files and adding lyrics, wouldn't it be great if you could take the fruits of your labor with you? The good news is, you can—all the info in an iTunes song file transfers over when you sync your iPod. Except, of course, if you have an iPod Shuffle, which lacks the whole screen thing needed to view images and text.

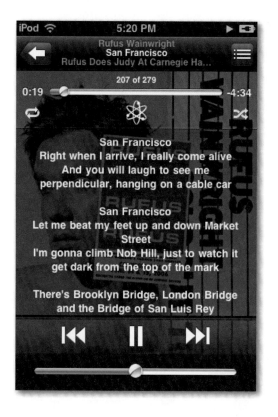

When you're out strolling with the iPod, press the center button while a song is playing to cycle through all the information about the song. After four or five taps, the lyrics appear on the iPod's screen, making it a handheld karaoke machine you can dance down the street with. Got an iPod Touch? Just tap the album cover on your screen to see the lyrics.

> **Tip** While you're clicking through iPod screens to get to your lyrics, check out the shortcut to shuffling that Apple has slipped into the menus. Right before you get to the lyrics screen, you get an option to shuffle songs or albums.

What iTunes Can Tell You About Your iPod

iTunes not only lets you decide which songs and videos end up on your iPod, it also helps keep your iPod's own internal software up to date, see how much space you have left on your player, and change your music, video, and podcast synchronization options.

When you connect your iPod to the computer it shows up in the iTunes Source list (in the Devices area), Click the iPod icon to see all your options. Each tab at the top of the screen lets you control a different kind of content, like Music, Photos, or Games.

Here on the Summary screen, iTunes tells you:

❶ The size of your iPod, its serial number, and if it's formatted for Windows or Macintosh.

❷ If your iPod has the latest software (or if it's having problems, the chance to reinstall its software).

❸ If your iPod is set to automatically synchronize with the iTunes library or have its contents updated manually by you. (Automatic means everything in iTunes ends up on your iPod—space permitting, of course; manual means you get to pick and choose.) If you have one of the new Nanos, you can turn on spoken-word prompts and hear your Nano recite things like menu names, song titles, and so on.

Use iTunes to See What's on Your iPod

iTunes gives you two ways to quickly see what digital goodies are loaded on your iPod. That info's important if you sync your iPod manually and can't remember if you copied a particular album or video over to the iPod. It's also helpful if you want to load a bunch of new movies, or other space-hogging files, and aren't sure how much room you've got left on your iPod.

- To see what's on your iPod, click the flippy triangle next to the iPod's icon in the iTunes Source list. Then click any category—Music, Movies, and so on—to have iTunes display all the stuff under the selected category.

- Click the iPod's icon and then click the Summary tab in the main window to see a color graphic displaying how much of your iPod is filled with audio, video, photos, applications, and so on. If you want more information than say, "12.5 gigabytes," click the colored bar itself to see the statistics change to the number of items in each category (like 440 photos or 3396 songs), or how many hours (even *days*) worth of each type of media your iPod is holding for you.

Capacity 7.01 GB	Audio 1.01 GB	Video 2.41 GB	Photos 170.9 MB	Apps 43.5 MB	Other 114.9 MB	Free 3.28 GB	Sync

Adjust Your iPod's Preferences with iTunes

Once your iPod's connected and showing up in iTunes, you can modify all the settings that control what goes on (and comes off) your media player. See those tabs in a row towards the top of iTunes? Click each one to get to those specific preferences. Here's what you'll find in each area (the tabs vary slightly depending on the type of iPod you've got):

❶ **Summary.** Key iPod hardware info here: Drive capacity, serial number, and software version (and a button to update the same when Apple releases a new version). The Options area lets you choose syncing options and whether to turn your iPod into a portable data drive for carrying around big files.

❷ **Music.** Click this tab to synchronize all songs and playlists—or just the ones you listen to the most.

❸ **Movies.** Full-length movies can take up a gigabyte or more of precious 'Pod space, so iTunes gives you the option of loading up all, selected, or even just unwatched films.

❹ **TV Shows.** As with Movies, you can selectively choose which TV Shows you want to bring along on your iPod.

❺ **Podcasts.** Your pal iTunes can automatically download the podcasts you've *subscribed* to through the iTunes Store (Chapter 7); here you can decide which ones you want to listen to on the go.

> **Tip** Both the iPod Nano and iTunes have features for the visually impaired to navigate music and other audio content by verbal cues instead of onscreen menus. In iTunes, on the Nano's Summary screen, turn on the checkbox next to "Enable spoken menus for accessibility". On the Nano itself, scroll to iPod→Settings→General→Spoken Menus. And if you want to control iTunes using the Mac's built-in VoiceOver software, and many screen-reader programs for Windows, pay a visit to: *www.apple.com/accessibility/itunes/vision.html*.

| Summary | Music | Movies | TV Shows | Podcasts | Photos | Contacts | Games |

Music

☑ Sync music
  ○ All songs and playlists
  ◉ Selected playlists:

    ☑ 🎵 Purchased
    ▼ ☐ 📁 Dinner Party playlists
    ☐ 🎵 Music Videos
    ☐ 🎵 My Top Rated
    ☐ 🎵 Top 25 Most Played
    ☑ 🎵 A Hot New Playlist
    ☐ 🎵 Audible
    ☑ 🎵 BBQ Mix

☑ Include music videos
☑ Display album artwork on your iPod

❻ Photos. The Classic, Nano, and Touch can all display little copies of your digital photos. Click this tab to select where you want iTunes to look for photos (like in iPhoto or Photoshop Elements) and which specific albums you want.

❼ Contacts. It's not just an all-purpose media player! The iPod is happy to carry copies of all addresses and phone numbers in your computer's address book (from Microsoft Outlook, the Mac OS X Address Book, and other programs). Scroll down the screen and there's an option to grab Outlook or iCal calendars, too.

This tab is called **Info** on the iPod Touch. Along with contacts and calendars, you can sync up Web browser bookmarks and email account settings from your computer. If you're a MobileMe subscriber, you can add your Touch to your collection of über-synced computers and iPhones to keep your info current across all your Internet-connected hardware.

❽ Games. You get a few basic built-in iPod games in your Extras menu, but if you've purchased *Pac-Man* or *Bejeweled* from the iTunes Store, you can decide here which ones to move to your iPod.

If you have a Touch, this tab is called **Applications**. It's where you select how many of those cool little programs you downloaded from the iTunes App Store will sync up with your iPod.

Load Songs on an iPod from More Than One Computer

iTunes' *Autosync* feature makes keeping your iPod up-to-date a total breeze, but there's a big catch: You can sync your iPod with only *one* computer. Lots of people have music scattered around multiple machines: a couple of different family Macs, an office PC and a home PC, and so on. If you want to load up your music from each one of these, you have to change the iPod to *manual management.* That's easy to do. Just connect the iPod, select it in the Source list, and then click the Summary tab in the iTunes window. Then:

- Scroll down to the Options area and turn on the checkbox next to "Manually manage music and videos". Click the Apply button in the bottom corner of iTunes to make the change.

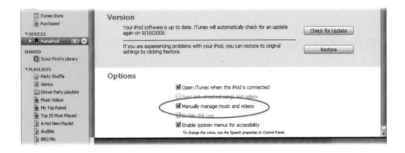

- Don't forget to manually eject the iPod from iTunes every time you want to remove it from your computer. (Manual update gives you total control, but as Uncle Ben said in *Spider-Man*, "With great power comes great responsibility.") Eject the iPod by either clicking the Eject button next to its name in the iTunes Source list or pressing press Ctrl+E (⌘-E) to properly free the player from the computer.

Tip Your iPod's Summary screen (in iTunes) shows whether the iPod is formatted for Mac or Windows. If you have a new Classic or Nano and want to use it with both a Mac and a PC, connect it to the PC first and have iTunes format the iPod for Windows. A Mac can read the Windows format just fine, but Windows won't recognize the Mac format without special software. The iPod Touch will talk to either computer, no matter which one you used it with first.

Manually Delete Music and Videos from the iPod

People who choose to autosync their iPods don't have to worry about dumping stuff off their players. They can choose which playlists and media to automatically copy over to the iPod—or they can just delete unwanted items out of iTunes and resync to wipe the same files off the player.

If you're a Manual Manager, you have to delete unwanted files yourself. (You can, however, have iTunes automatically update your podcast subscriptions for you; see Chapter 7 for more about podcasts.)

❶ To delete files from your iPod, connect it to the computer, and click the iPod icon in the Source list.

❷ Click the flippy triangle next to the iPod icon to get to the media library you want to clean up. If you want to delete some songs, for example, click the Music icon.

❸ In the list that appears on the right side of iTunes, select the unwanted songs and press the Delete key on the keyboard. This removes the files from your iPod, but doesn't whack them out of the iTunes library.

Where iTunes Stores Your Files

Behind its steely silver-framed window, iTunes has a very precise system for keeping your music, movies, and everything else you've added organized. Inside its own iTunes folder on your hard drive (which, unless you've moved it, is in My Documents→My Music→iTunes [Home→Music→iTunes]), the program stores all your files and song information. (If you're running Windows Vista, your iTunes folder is at User→<username>→Music→iTunes.)

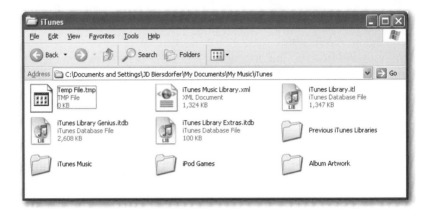

Inside this iTunes folder is your iTunes Library file, a database that contains the names of all the songs, playlists, videos, and other content you've added to iTunes. Be very careful not to move or delete this file if you happen to be poking around in the iTunes folder. If iTunes can't find its Library file, it gives a little sigh and just creates a new one—a new one which doesn't have a record of all your songs and other media goodies.

Even if you accidentally delete the Library file, your music is still on the computer—even if iTunes doesn't know it. That's because all the song files are actually stored in the iTunes Music folder, which is also inside the main iTunes folder. You may lose your custom playlist if your Library file goes missing, but you can always add the music files back (File→"Add to Library") and recreate your library.

Move the iTunes Music Folder to an External Drive

Media libraries grow large and hard drives can seem to shrink as thousands of songs and hundreds of videos begin to fill up the space. You may, in fact, be thinking of getting a big external hard drive to use for iTunes storage. That's just dandy, but you need to make sure iTunes knows what you intend to do.

If you rudely drag the iTunes Music folder to a different place without telling iTunes, it thinks the songs and videos in your collection are gone. The next time you start the program, you'll find it empty. (While iTunes remains empty but calm, *you* may have heart palpitations as you picture your media collection vanishing in a puff of bytes.)

To move the iTunes Music folder to a new drive, just let the program know where you're putting it. Move the folder to the desired location, then, in the Preferences box (Ctrl+comma/⌘-comma), click the Advanced icon or tab. In the area labeled "iTunes Music folder location", click the Change button, and navigate to the place where you moved the folder. Finally, click OK.

Copy Your Music From iPod to iTunes

To prevent rampant piracy across the seven seas of Musicdom, the data transfer between iTunes and the iPod was originally designed as a one-way trip—you could copy music *to* a connected iPod, but not *from* it to the computer. This is still pretty much Apple's way, although you can now copy iTunes Store purchases from the iPod to iTunes; Chapter 7 has the details for this handy trick.

But there are times when perfectly honest people need to get their songs off the iPod—like when your computer dies and takes its iTunes library with it.

The Web is full of tips and tricks for harvesting content off an iPod and getting it back into iTunes, often by fiddling with system settings in Windows or Mac OS X. These methods can vary based on which iPod and which version of the operating system are involved. Thankfully, there's also The Shareware Option. Several helpful folks have developed free or inexpensive programs to copy content on your iPod back to the computer:

- **TouchCopy.** The program costs $25 but it works with Mac OS X and Windows—and all iPod models. (*www.wideanglesoftware.com/touchcopy*)

- **YamiPod.** A free program that can run off the iPod itself and exports music back to Windows, Mac, and Linux systems. (*www.yamipod.com*)

- **SharePod.** This freeware program for Windows can copy music and videos back to the PC and also edit playlists, artwork, and song tags (labels) as well. (*www.getsharepod.com*)

- **iPodAccess.** This one works with all iPods and is available for $20 in either Mac or Windows versions. (*www.findleydesigns.com/ipodaccess*)

- **Senuti.** The names makes sense when you realize it's iTunes spelled backwards. Senuti, pictured at right, is handy freeware for the Mac that lets you copy all (or just some) of the music on the iPod back to iTunes. (*www.fadingred.org/senuti*)

Back Up Your iTunes Files

If your hard drive dies and takes the whole iTunes folder with it, you lose your music. This can be especially painful if you paid for lots of songs and videos from the iTunes Store, because Apple won't let you re-download new copies. Luckily, iTunes gives you a super simple way to back up your iTunes files onto a CD or DVD.

❶ In iTunes, choose File→Library→"Back Up to Disc".

❷ In the box that pops up, choose what you want to back up—everything or just items you paid for in the iTunes Store. Later, after you've backed up for the first time, you can turn on the checkbox for backing up only new stuff that you've added since last backing up.

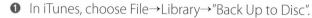

❸ Have a stack of discs ready to feed into your computer's disc drive. Depending on the size of your library, you may need several CDs (which store up to 700 megabytes of data each) or DVDs (which pack in at least 4.7 gigabytes of files per disc). You'll get nagged by iTunes to feed it a new disc when it's filled up the first one.

If you ever need to use your backup, open iTunes and put in one of those discs to start restoring your files. Remember, there's nothing really exciting about file backups—until you have to use them to save the day.

The Power of Playlists

A playlist is a group of songs from your iTunes library that you've decided should go together. It can be made up of pretty much any collection of tunes arranged in any order. For example, if you're having a party, you can make a playlist out of the current Top 40 and dance music in your iTunes library. If you're in a 1960s Brit Girl Pop mood, you can whip together the hits of Dusty Springfield, Lulu, and Petula Clark. Some people may question your taste if you, say, mix tracks from *La Bohème* with Queen's *A Night at the Opera*, but hey—it's *your* playlist.

Creating playlists has become something of an art form, especially since the iPod arrived in 2001. Several books filled with sample playlists have been published. Academics around the world are writing papers about group dynamics and cultural identity after studying how people make playlists—and which ones they choose to share with others. You can publish your own playlists in the iTunes Store (Chapter 7) so others can witness your mixing prowess. And some nightclubs even invite people to hook up their iPods and share their playlists with the dance-floor audience.

And even if you don't have time to make your own playlists, Apple lends you an expert hand. The Genius feature lets you create one-click mixes of music that actually sounds like it's supposed to go together.

Now that you know what a playlist is and how people use them, it's time to get cracking and make one or 42 of your own.

Make a New Playlist in iTunes

To create a playlist, press Ctrl+N (⌘-N). You can also choose File→New Playlist or click the + button below the Source list.

All freshly minted playlists start out with the impersonal name "untitled playlist." Fortunately, its renaming rectangle is open and highlighted—just type a better name: Cardio Workout, Hits of the Highland Lute, or whatever you want to call it. As you add them, your playlists alphabetize themselves in the Playlists area.

Once you've created and named this spanking new playlist, you're ready to add your songs or videos. You can do this in several different ways, so choose the method you like best.

Playlist-Making Method #1

❶ If this is your first playlist, opening the playlist into its own window makes it easy to see what's going on. You get your empty playlist in one window, and your full library in another. To make this happen, just double-click the new playlist's icon in the Source list.

❷ Now drag the song titles you want from the main iTunes window over to the new playlist window. (Make sure you've clicked the Music icon in the Source list to see all your songs.) Drag songs one at a time, or grab a bunch by selecting tracks as you go: Ctrl+click (⌘-click) each title.

Playlist-Making Method #2

❶ Some folks don't like multiple windows. No problem. You can add songs to a playlist by dragging tunes to the playlist's icon right from the main iTunes window.

❷ Tip: If you start accumulating lots of playlists you may need to scroll down to get to your new playlist.

Playlist-Making Method #3

❶ You can also pick and choose songs in your library, selecting tracks as you go by Ctrl+clicking (⌘-clicking) each title.

❷ Then choose File→New Playlist From Selection, or press Ctrl+Shift+N (⌘+Shift+N). All the songs you selected immediately appear in a brand-new playlist.

Don't worry about clogging up your hard drive. When you drag a song title onto a playlist, you don't *copy* the song; you're just giving iTunes instructions about where to find the files. In essence, you're creating an *alias* or *shortcut* to the original. That means you can have the same song on several different playlists.

That nice iTunes even gives you some playlists of its own devising, like "Top 25 Most Played" and "Purchased" (a convenient place to find all your iTunes Store goodies listed in one place).

Change an Existing Playlist

If you change your mind about a playlist's tune order, just drag the song titles up or down within the playlist window.

You can also drag more songs into a playlist or delete individual titles if you find your playlist needs pruning. (Click the song in the playlist window and then hit Delete or Backspace. When iTunes asks you to confirm your decision, click Yes.) Remember, deleting a song from a playlist doesn't delete it from your music library—it just removes the title from that particular *playlist*. (You can get rid of a song for good only by pressing Delete or Backspace when the Library's *Music* icon is selected.)

You can quickly add a song to an existing playlist right from the main iTunes window, no matter which view you happen to be using: Select the song, Ctrl+click (⌘-click) it, and then, in the pop-up menu, choose "Add to Playlist". Scroll to the playlist you want to use and then let go of the mouse button to add the track to that playlist.

If you want to see how many playlists contain a certain song, select the track, Ctrl+click (⌘-click) it, and choose "Show in Playlist" in the pop-up menu.

Add a Playlist to Your iPod

Adding that fabulous new playlist to your iPod doesn't take any heavy lifting on your part. In fact, if your iPod is set to autosync with iTunes, the only thing you need to do is grab your USB cable and plug in your iPod. Once iTunes recognizes the iPod, it copies any new playlists you've created right over.

You can also tell iTunes to sync different playlists to different iPods—helpful if you're in a multiple-iPod-owning household and you all share the same computer and iTunes library. Just plug in your iPod, select it in the Source list, and then click the Music tab. In the Sync Music area, click the button for "Selected playlists" and then turn on the checkboxes for the playlists you want *your* iPod to grab from the collection in iTunes.

If you manually manage the syncing process, adding new playlists is a total drag, literally—dragging is all you have to do. With your iPod connected, click the playlists icons you want to transfer and drag them onto the iPod's icon. That's it.

Note See that arrow at the end of your playlist? Click it and you have the option to either publish that very playlist as an iMix in the iTunes Store—or send the available tracks as gifted music to a pal. You"ll never run out of shopportunities with iTunes! Chapter 7 has the details on how to spend time (and money) in the Store.

Delete a Playlist

The party's over and you want to get rid of that iTunes playlist. Start by clicking it in the Source list and then pressing Backspace (Delete). iTunes presents you with a warning box, double-checking that you really want to vaporize the playlist. (Again, this maneuver just zaps the playlist itself, not all the stored songs you had in it. Those remain available in the main iTunes window.)

If you have your iPod set to autosync, any playlists you delete from iTunes will disappear the next time you plug in and sync your player.

If you manually manage your iPod and all its contents, connect the player and spin open the flippy triangle next to its name in the Source list. That gives you a look at all its libraries and playlists. Click the one you want to dump and hit the Backspace (Delete) key on the keyboard.

Make an On-The-Go Playlist on an iPod Nano or Classic

Sometimes you're out with your iPod, and you get the urge to hear a bunch of songs on different albums one after the other. Good news: You can create a playlist right on your iPod, and have it sync back into iTunes the next time you connect:

❶ Scroll through your iPod until you get to the title of the first song you want to add to the playlist.

❷ Hold down the iPod's center button for a few seconds until a new set of menus appear. Choose "Add to On-the-Go".

❸ Scroll to the next song and repeat the process.

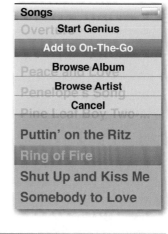

❹ When you're done adding songs, press the iPod's menu button until you get to the Music menu; go to Playlists→On-The-Go. Under "On-The-Go", you see the number of songs you just compiled. Press the Select button to see the song titles.

❺ If you like what you see, scroll up to "Save Playlist" and click the center button. (If you don't like what you see, choose "Clear Playlist" to dump the songs and start over.)

Your freshly inspired playlist now appears in your Playlists menu as On-The-Go 1. The next one you make and save will be On-The-Go 2, and so on. When you reconnect the iPod to iTunes, you can click the names and change them to something peppier—or more descriptive.

Make and Edit On-The-Go Playlists on the iPod Touch

Nanos and Classics aren't the only iPods to supply you with playlist fun on the run. The iPod Touch has its own version of the On-The-Go playlist as well. To make one, all you need is some songs and a finger.

Here's how:

- **Creating an On-The-Go Playlist.** Tap the Music icon on the Touch Home screen. Tap Playlists. At the top of the Playlists screen, tap On-The-Go.

  Now a master list of all your songs appears. Each time you see one worth adding, tap its name (or the + button). You can also tap one of the icons at the bottom, like Playlists, Artists, or Albums, to find the stuff you want. At the top of every list is an "Add All Songs" option that does just what it says—adds all the songs listed to your OTG playlist.

  When you're finished, tap Done. Your playlist is ready to play, just like any playlist.

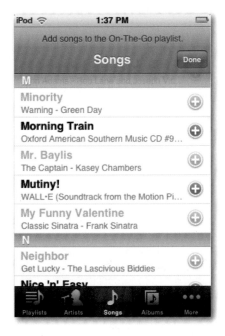

- **Editing the On-The-Go Playlist.** On the Playlists screen, tap On-The-Go; on the next screen, tap Edit. Here you're offered a Clear Playlist command, which (after a confirmation request) empties the list completely.

  You also see the universal iPod Touch Delete symbol (⊖). Tap it, and then tap the Delete confirmation button on the right side, to remove a song from the playlist.

  To add more songs to the list, tap the ⊕ button at the top left. Each time you see a song worth adding, tap it. Finally, note the "grip strip" at the right edge of the screen (≡). With your finger, drag these handles up or down to rearrange the songs in your OTG playlist. When your editing job is complete, tap Done.

Make a Genius Playlist in iTunes

Playlists are fun to make, but occasionally you just don't have the time or energy. If this is the case, call in the expert—the iTunes Genius. With the Genius feature, you click any song that you're in the mood for and iTunes brings back a playlist of 25 to 100 songs that it thinks go well with the one you picked.

The first time you use it, Genius asks permisson to go through your music collection and gather song information. Then it uploads the data to Apple. When your information has been analyzed (by software) and anonymously added to a big giant database of everybody else's song info (for better suggestions), the Genius is ready for duty. Here's the procedure, step-by-step:

❶ Click a song title in your libary.

❷ Click the Genius button ⬚ at the bottom of iTunes. If you're playing the song already, click the Genius icon in the iTunes display window.

❸ iTunes presents you with your new playlist in a flash.

❹ Use the buttons at the top of the Genius window to adjust the number of songs in the playlist, refresh it with new songs if you want a different mix, and—best of all—save the playlist permanently.

Based On: **Pine Leaf Boy Two-Step by Pine Leaf Boys**		Limit to: (25 songs ⬍) (Refresh) (Save Playlist)	
▶ ▲ **Name**	**Artist**	**Album**	**T**
1 ☑ Pine Leaf Boy Two-Step ◉	Pine Leaf Boys ◉	La musique ◉	
2 ☑ Zydeco Gris Gris	Beausoleil	The Big Easy	
3 ☑ Wagon Wheel	Old Crow Medicine Show	O C M S	
4 ☑ The Night They Drove Old Dixie Down	Joan Baez	The Joan Baez Country Mus...	
5 ☑ The Hallelujah Chorus	The Roches	Keep on Doing	

The Genius doesn't work if it doesn't have enough information about a song—or if there aren't enough similar songs available to match it with. In that case, pick another tune. If you frequently add new music to your library and want to get it in the mix, inform the Genius at Store→Update Genius.

And if you happen to have the Genius Sidebar panel open in your iTunes window (Chapter 4), the Genius cheerfully presents you with a list of other songs that you can buy right there to round out your listening experience.

> **Note** If you declined iTunes' initial offer to activate the Genius, you can summon it again by choosing Store→"Turn on Genius". And if you're regretting your choice to invite the Genius into your iTunes home, kick him out for good by visiting the same menu and choosing Turn Off Genius.

Make a Genius Playlist on the iPod

You may get so hooked on making Genius playlists in iTunes that you never want to leave your computer. Your friends will start wondering where you are. But before your face ends up on a milk carton, consider this: You can also make Genius playlists on the iPod itself when you're out and about. You just need to have the latest model Touch, Nano, or Classic.

To use your portable pocket Genius, though, you first have to set it up and upload your information from iTunes to Apple's servers, as described on the previous page. But you've probably already done that by now, so here's how to make the Genius do your bidding when you're away from the computer.

❶ On a Nano or Classic, select a song and hold down the iPod's center button for a few seconds until the menu appears; choose "Start Genius". On the Touch, tap Music→Playlists→Genius and then tap the song you want Genius to use from the list.

❷ If you don't like the mix, select or tap the Refesh option at the top of the screen to get new tunes.

❸ If you love the work of Genius, select or tap the Save option at the top of the screen.

As in iTunes, Genius playlists are titled with the name of the song you originally chose as the foundation for your mix. When you sync the iPod with iTunes, the traveling Genius playlists get copied back over to iTunes.

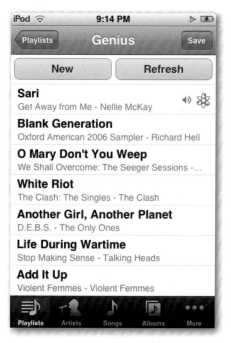

Make Playlist Folders

If you like to have a playlist or five for every occasion, but find your iTunes Source list is getting crowded, iTunes lets you store multiple playlists inside convenient folders.

❶ To add a folder to your Source list, click the Source list's Library icon and then choose File→New Playlist Folder.

❷ A new "untitled folder" appears, inviting you to change its name to something more original, like Dinner Party Playlists.

❸ Drag any playlists you want to store inside the folder onto its icon.

If the whole family shares one computer, folders can give each person a tidy receptacle to store his or her personal playlists. Folders are also great for storing a bunch of playlists that go well together. That way, when you select the folder and hit play, iTunes plays all the folder's songs consecutively.

Note Great news for iTunes Veterans. Back in Ye Olden Days, iTunes used to dump all your playlists-inside-a-folder into one massive playlist (using the folder name) onto your iPod. No more. Now, once you sync your iPod, you end up with a folder's individual playlists all right there on your iPod.

Smart Playlists: Another Way for iTunes to Assemble Your Playlists

As cool as the Genius is, sometimes you want a little more manual control over what goes into your automatically generated music mixes. This is where Smart Playlists rise to the occasion.

Once you give it some guidelines, a *Smart Playlist* can go sniffing through your music library and come up with its own mix. A Smart Playlist even keeps tabs on the music that comes and goes from your library and adjusts itself on the fly.

You might tell one Smart Playlist to assemble 45 minutes worth of songs that you've rated higher than four stars but rarely listen to, and another to play your most-often-played songs from the 1980s. The Smart Playlists you create are limited only by your imagination.

❶ **To start a Smart Playlist, press Ctrl+Alt+N (Option-⌘-N) or choose File→New Smart Playlist.** A Smart Playlist box opens: It sports a purple gear-shaped icon next to its name in the Source list (a regular playlist has a blue icon with a music note icon in it).

❷ **Give iTunes detailed instructions about what you want to hear.** You can select a few artists you like and have iTunes leave off the ones you're not in the mood for, pluck songs that only fall within a certain genre or year, and so on. To add multiple criteria click the plus (+) button.

❸ **Turn on the "Live updating" checkbox.** This tells iTunes to keep this playlist updated as your collection, ratings, and play count change.

❹ **To edit an existing Smart Playlist, right-click (Control-click) the playlist's name.** Then choose Edit Smart Playlist.

A Smart Playlist is a dialogue between you and iTunes: You tell it what you want in as much detail as you want, and the program whips up a playlist according to your instructions.

You can even instruct a Smart Playlist to pull tracks from your current Genius playlist. Just click the + button to add a field, choose Playlist as another criteria, and select Genius from the list of available playlist choices.

> **Tip** When you press Shift (Option), the + button at the bottom of the iTunes window turns into a gear icon. Click this gear button to quickly launch the Smart Playlist creation box.

Party Shuffle: When You Want to Play DJ

The standard iTunes song shuffle feature can be inspiring or embarrassing, depending on which songs the program happens to play. Party Shuffle lets *you* control which songs iTunes selects when it's shuffling at your next wingding. It also shows you what's already been played and what's coming up in the mix, so you'll know what to expect.

❶ **Click the Party Shuffle icon in the Playlists area of the iTunes Source list.** Now you see a new pane at the very bottom of iTunes.

❷ **Use the Source pop-up menu to select a music source for the mix.** You can use either an existing playlist or your whole library.

❸ **If you don't like the song list that iTunes proposes, click the Refresh button at the bottom right of the iTunes window.** iTunes generates a new list of songs for your consideration.

❹ **Arrange the songs if you feel like it.** You can manually add songs, delete them from the playlist, or rearrange the playing order. To add songs, click the Source list's Music icon and then drag your selected tunes onto the Party Shuffle icon.

❺ **Click the Play button.** And let the music play on.

Three Kinds of Discs You Can Create with iTunes

If you want to record a certain playlist on a CD for posterity—or for the Mr. Shower CD player in the bathroom—iTunes gives you the power to burn. In fact, it can create any of three kinds of discs:

- **Standard audio CDs.** This is the best option: If your computer has a CD burner, it can serve as your own private record label. iTunes can record selected sets of songs, no matter what the original sources, onto a blank CD. When it's all over, you can play the burned CD on  any standard CD player, just like the ones from Best Buy—but this time, you hear only the songs you like, in the order you like, with all the annoying ones eliminated.

- **MP3 CDs.** A standard audio CD contains high-quality, enormous song files in the AIFF format. An *MP3* compact disc, however, is a data CD that contains music files in the MP3 format. Because MP3 songs are much smaller than the AIFF files, many more of them fit in the standard 650 or 700 MB of space on a recordable CD. The bottom line? Instead of 74 or 80 minutes of music, a CD full of MP3 files can store *10 to 12 hours* of tunes. The downside? Older CD players may not be able to play these CDs.

- **Backup CDs or DVDs.** If your computer can play and record both CDs and/or DVDs, you have another option. iTunes can back up your collection by copying it to a CD or DVD. (The disc won't play in any kind of player, of course; it's just a glorified backup disk for restoration when something goes wrong with your hard drive.) Chapter 5 tells you how to use data discs to back up your iTunes library.

To see if your disc drive is compatible with iTunes, select a playlist and click the Burn Disc button on the iTunes window to get the Burn Settings box. If your drive name is listed next to "CD Burner," iTunes recognizes it.

> **Note** Even if you've got a DVD drive, you still see it listed next to the label "CD Burner."

Burn a Playlist to a CD

Making a CD out of your favorite playlist takes just a few simple steps with iTunes: Get your blank disc ready and click along.

❶ **Select the playlist you want to burn.** Check to make sure your songs are in the order you want them; drag any tune up or down to reorder.

❷ **When you're ready to roll, choose File→Library→"Burn Playlist to Disc" (or click the Burn Disc button at the bottom of the iTunes window).** When the Burn Settings box pops up, pick the type of disc you want to create (see the previous page for your choices).

❸ **Insert a blank disc into your computer's drive when prompted.** If your computer's got a CD platter that slides out, push it back in. Then sit back as iTunes handles things.

iTunes prepares to record the disc, which may take a few minutes. In addition to prepping the disc for recording, iTunes has to convert the music files (if you're burning an audio CD) to the standard format used by audio CDs.

Once iTunes has taken care of business, it lets you know that it's now burning the disc. Again, depending on the speed of your computer and disc burner, as well as the size of your playlist, the recording process could take several minutes. When the disc is done, iTunes pipes up with a musical flourish. Eject the disc and off you go. But if you want to make a nice looking CD cover...

Print Playlists and Snazzy CD Covers

You used to have to do a lot of gymnastics just to print a nice-looking song list that would fit into a CD case. But with iTunes, all you need to do is choose File→Print, select a preformatted option, and then click the Print button.

The Print dialog box is *full* of choices.

- **CD jewel case insert.** You can print out a perfectly sized insert for a CD jewel case, complete with song list on the left and a miniature mosaic of all your album artwork on the right—or just a plain list of songs on a solid color background. (If you choose to make a CD insert, your resulting printout even comes with handy crop marks to guide your X-Acto blade when trimming it down to size.)

- **Song listing.** If you want something simpler, you can opt for a straight-forward list of all the songs on the playlist. This option is also great for printing out a list of all the podcasts you currently have in your iTunes library—just click the Podcasts icon in the Source list, click the "Song list-ing" option, and print away.

- **Album listing.** You can also print a list of all the albums that have con-tributed songs to your playlist, complete with album title, artist name, and the songs' titles and times for each track culled from that album.

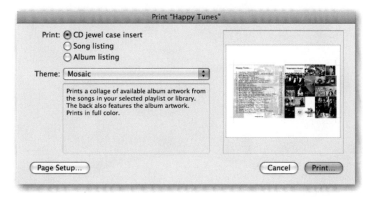

Want to use one of your own personal photos for the cover of your CD case? Start by adding the artwork of your choice to a track (Chapter 5). When you're ready to print, select that track on the playlist and then choose File→Print→"CD jewel case insert"→Theme: Single Cover to place your photo front and center. This method also works great if you're looking to create jewel case inserts that look just like the ones that come with commercial CDs.

Shop the iTunes Store

People have been downloading music from the Internet since the 1990s, from sites that were legal and others that were, well, not so much. Music fans loved the convenience, but record companies saw potential profits slipping down millions of modem lines. They fought back by suing file-sharing services and other software companies for aiding and abetting copyright infringement.

The need for a legal music download site was obvious, but most early efforts resulted in skimpy song catalogs and confusing usage rights. Things changed dramatically in April 2003, when the iTunes Music Store went online. Apple made deals with several major record companies to sell digital versions of popular songs for 99 cents a pop—and you could instantly transfer and play the tunes on your iPod or burn them to a CD. Things have gotten even better since.

Now simply called the iTunes Store, you can find millions of songs, plus full-length movies, TV shows, audio books, podcasts, iPod Touch applications, video games, music videos, and more on its virtual shelves. It's all custom-tailored for the iPod, and best of all, once you download a title, it's yours to keep. This chapter shows you how to find and use what you're looking for, and get more out of The Store.

Getting to the iTunes Store

Compared to paying for gas, fighting traffic, and finding a parking spot at the mall, getting to the iTunes
Store is easy. All you need is an Internet connection
and a copy of iTunes running on your computer. Once
you're online and looking at iTunes, you can either:

❶ Click the iTunes Store icon in the Source list.

❷ Click the icon in the lower-right corner of the
iTunes window (circled) to slide open the Genius
Sidebar, where any *Buy* button or song title you
click will sweep you into the Store. (This option's
available only when you're playing your own
music and *don't* have the iTunes Store selected.)

The first method lands you squarely on the Store's
main page. You can start wandering around from
there, clicking on what looks good.

The second method is a little more targeted to what
you're currently listening to. If you're chilling out to
some Etta Baker, the Sidebar rounds up more of her
tracks, plus recommendations for works by similar artists. Preview suggested songs by clicking the musical
note icon in front of the track's title. The Buy button
is there waiting for your impulse purchase, making it
extremely easy to run up your credit-card tab.

If you have an iPod Touch and are in range of a wireless network connection, you have a third way to get
to the Store: over the airwaves, as explained on the
next page.

Tip Even if you're still paddling around the Net on a dial-up modem, you can shop for
audio files in the Store. But you may want to shop first and download everything
at the end of your session. That's because you may have a few hours of download
time ahead of you as your purchases squeeze through the telephone line. See "A
Tip for Dial-Up Music Lovers" later in this chapter.

Shop the iTunes Wi-Fi Music Store

Owners of the iPod Touch don't even *need* a computer to shop the iTunes Store—these lucky souls can tap their way right into the iTunes inventory over a wireless Internet connection. Many Wi-Fi-enabled Starbucks coffee shops also let you tap into the iTunes Store to browse and buy music, including whatever track is currently playing right there at Starbucks.

When using the iTunes Wi-Fi Music Store, there's one major thing to remember. You need to have signed into your iTunes Store account (on your computer) the last time you synced up your Touch. (If you don't have an account yet, you'll learn how to get one in a few pages.)

Now, to buy music when you're out and about—and in the mood to shop:

❶ Tap the iTunes icon on the iPod Touch's Home screen. Make sure you have a Wi-Fi connection; see Chapter 11 for guidance on making that happen.

❷ The Store appears on screen. Tap your way through the categories like "What's Hot" until you find an album or song that interests you. (Tap an album title to see all its songs.)

❸ Tap a song to hear a 30-second preview.

❹ For targeted shopping, tap the Search button at the bottom of the window to call up the Search box. Use the Touch's onscreen keyboard to enter what you're looking for.

❺ To buy and download a song or album, tap the price on screeen, then tap Buy Now.

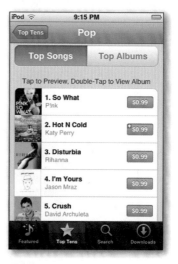

❻ Type in your iTunes Store password and let the download begin. You can check the status of your purchase-in-progress by tapping the Downloads button, which also lets you pause your download if you need to.

You now have some brand new music ready to play on your Touch—the new tracks are now on the Purchased playlist.

To get those freshly harvested songs back into the iTunes library on your computer, sync up the Touch when you get home. The tracks pop up in a new iTunes playlist called "Purchased on Touchy" (or whatever you named your wireless iPod this week).

An Overview of the Store's Layout

The iTunes Store is jam-packed with digital merchandise, all neatly filed under category links along the upper-left side of the main window. Click a link to go to that section of the store: Music, Movies, TV Shows, Podcasts, and so on.

Other links along the left side include Top TV Episodes, Top Movie Rentals, Top Movie Sales, Top Music Videos, Top Podcasts: all the most popular downloads in the Store at the moment. The right side of the screen displays lists of Top Songs, Top Albums, Top Ringtones, Top Audiobooks, and Top Podcasts. Tops for both paid and free Apps (programs for the Touch) are listed as well.

The center part of the window highlights the Store's latest specials and releases. Free song downloads and other offers appear here, too.

If you're looking for a specific item, the Search box (upper-right corner) lets you home in on your quest by entering titles, artist names, or other searchable info.

The right side of the window has a helpful box of Quick Links to your Account settings, buying and redeeming iTunes Gift Certificates, technical support, and more.

Navigate the Aisles of the iTunes Store

You navigate the iTunes Store aisles just like a Web browser. Most song and artist names are hyperlinked—that is, click their names, or album cover images, to see what tracks are included.

Click the upper-left corner's Back button to return to the page you were just on, or click the button with the small house on it (circled below) to jump to the Store's home page.

When you find a performer you're interested in, click the name to see a list of available songs or albums. If you click an album name, all the songs available from it appear below, in the Details window. Double-click a track title to hear a 30-second snippet. Short previews of items in the Store's audio book and video collection are also available, as are movie trailers.

When browsing the store, you may see a small, gray, circular icon bearing a white arrow in some columns of the Details window. That's the "More Info This Way!" button. (You also get the Little Gray Arrows on tracks in your own library because iTunes wastes no opportunity to get you to visit the Store.) Click the arrow to jump to a page bearing details about the subject, like a discography page, or the main page of artists for the genre listed.

More info button

Set Up an iTunes Store Account

Before you can buy any of the cool stuff you see in the Store, you need to set up an account with Apple. To do so, click the "Sign In" button on the upper-right corner of the iTunes window.

> **Tip** America Online members can use their AOL screen names to log into the Store, and then pay for their purchases using their AOL Wallet. See AOL's Help section if you need assistance opening your Wallet.

If you've ever bought or registered an Apple product on the company's Web site, signed up for an AppleCare tech-support plan, have a MobileMe membership, or used another Apple service, you probably already have the requisite Apple ID. All you have to do is remember the ID (usually your email address) and password.

If you've never had an Apple ID, click Create New Account. The iTunes Store Welcome presents you with the three steps you need to follow:

❶ Agree to the terms for using the Store and buying music.

❷ Create an Apple Account.

❸ Supply a credit card or PayPal account number and billing address.

As your first step to creating an Apple Account, you must read and agree to the long scrolling legal agreement on the first screen. The 18-page statement informs you of your rights and responsibilities as an iTunes Store and App Store customer. (It boils down to this: *Thou shalt not download an album, burn it to CD, and then sell bootleg copies of it at your local convenience store.* and *Third-party crashware apps are not our fault.*)

Click the Agree button to move on to step 2. Here, you create an Apple ID, password, and secret question and answer. If you later have to click the "Forgot Password?" button in the Store sign-in box, this is the question you'll have to answer to prove that you're you. Apple also requests that you type in your birthday to help verify your identity.

On the third and final screen, provide a valid credit card number with a billing address. Instead of a credit card, you can also use a PayPal account for iTunes purchases.

Click Done. You've got yourself an Apple Account. From now on, you can log into the iTunes Store by clicking the "Sign In" button in the upper-right corner of the iTunes window.

Change the Information in Your Apple Account

You can change your billing address, switch the credit card you have on file for Store purchases, or edit other information in your Apple Account without calling Apple. Just launch iTunes, click the Store icon in the Source list, and then sign in to your account by clicking the Sign In button in the upper-right corner of the screen.

---

iTunes

Enter Password for "jude@echo.com"

To view your account information, enter your password and click View Account. To prevent others from using your account to buy music, click Sign Out.

Apple ID:

jude@echo.com   Example: steve@me.com

Password:

••••••   Forgot Password?

AOL

? | Sign Out   View Account | Cancel

Once you've signed in, you'll see your account name (email address). Click it. In the box that pops up, re-enter your password and click View Account. If you want to change your password or secret identity-proving question, click the Edit Account Info button. To change your billing address or credit card information, click the Edit Payment Information button. You can also deauthorize all the computers that can play songs purchased with this account (more on when and why you'd want to do *that* later).

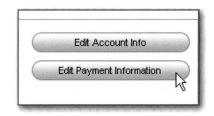

Edit Account Info

Edit Payment Information

And there are other account settings you can change here, too, like the nickname that appears when you post a customer review in the Store. You can also turn on the My iTunes feature, which lets you put widgets and news feeds on your blog or Facebook profile showing all the things you've been snapping up in the Store lately.

Note By the way, any changes you make to your Apple Account through iTunes affect other programs or services you then use with your account, like ordering pictures with iPhoto (Mac owners only).

A Tip for Dial-Up Music Lovers

The fact is, the iTunes Store works best with a high-speed Internet connection. Thanks to Apple's 1-Click option (see the top radio button in the image below), iTunes can instantly download a selected track as soon as you click the Buy Song button. That's a quick and painless experience for high speeders, but not so much fun for dial-up folks who have to wait for each track to download, bit by painfully slow bit.

If you have a dial-up modem and want a smoother shopping experience, iTunes has a setting that may help. You can find it on the Store tab of the iTunes Preferences box (Ctrl+comma/⌘-comma).

❶ **Buy using a Shopping Cart.** Now all songs you buy pile up until the end of your shopping session; then iTunes downloads them all at once when you click the Shopping Cart icon in your iTunes Source list (and then click Buy Now). This way, you can go off and do something productive while the stack of tracks squeezes through the dial-up connection.

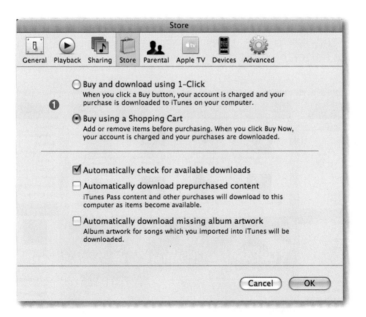

Find Music by Genre

The main page of the iTunes Store can be a bit overwhelming, especially if you just want to slip in and buy a few Celtic music tracks or browse the latest additions to the Classical section. To quickly find music by genre, click the Genres drop-down menu conveniently located next to the Music link.

On this handy menu, twenty different musical genres await you, from Alternative to World, with Hip-Hop/Rap, Latin, Jazz, Reggae, and Rock in between. You'll also find a section for Children's Music.

Select one of the genre options and the middle section of the Store window displays all the latest albums in that category, including the newest releases and songs just added to the ever-growing iTunes catalog. The list of top songs, albums, and music videos along the side of the window also changes to reflect the most popular downloads for the genre you've chosen.

Buy a Song or Album

Clicking any album name shows you a list of all the songs available from the record. To purchase any tune, click the Buy Song button in the Price column. You also have the option, in most cases, to buy the whole album with the Buy Album button. See that plus sign (circled below) by some tracks? That's an iTunes Plus track—a higher-fidelity file at the same price as a regular song.

When you download an album, or even just one song, it's accompanied by a color picture of the album cover, which appears in iTunes when you're playing the song, or on the color screen of your iPod. Many new albums are also starting to include short music videos and interactive electronic booklets (think liner notes gone digital).

![iTunes Store screenshot showing The Ultimate Ella Fitzgerald album with track listing and Buy Song buttons]

Once you click that Buy Song button, an alert box appears asking if you really want to buy the item you just clicked. Click the glowing Buy button to confirm your purchase decision, or Cancel if you suddenly remember that your credit card is a bit close to the limit this month. Once you click Buy, the download begins and you soon have a new bit of music in your iTunes library.

> **Tip** Buy three songs off an album and wish later you'd just bought the whole thing? If it's within six months of your original purchase, click the Complete My Album link on the main Store page. You get whisked into a screen that lets you download the rest of the tracks—all for a price that's less than paying for each remaining song.

Buy Movies or Videos

To buy video content, just click the link on the Store's main page for the type you want—a music video, a movie, or a TV show. Apple's full-length movie library is small but growing. You'll see titles like *Pirates of the Caribbean*, *National Treasure*, and a handful of Disney classics like *Dumbo* and *The Little Mermaid*. Compared to little ol' song files, movies can take up a ton of hard drive space—a full gigabyte or more—so be prepared for a download time of 30 minutes or more, depending on your Internet connection.

> **Tip** If you want to watch a movie but not own it, check the flick's Store page to see if it's available for rental. Rentals cost less than $5 and download just like regular iTunes Store–purchased movies that you can play on your iPod or computer. You have 30 days to start watching the rental and 24 hours to finish it, but it means never having to wait for Netflix—or slog to the video store in the rain.

Dozens of old and new TV classics are also available, including episodes from *Heroes*, *The Daily Show*, and *Grey's Anatomy*. You can buy single episodes or entire seasons at once. Sign up for a Season Pass and you get each new show automatically as it's released. TV shows are big files, too: one 30-minute episode of *30 Rock*, for instance, is close to 300 megabytes.

Once you purchase and download the files from the iTunes Store—just click the Buy button next to the title you want—they land in your iTunes Library.

Many videos in the iTunes Store come in high-definition as well as standard definition. The HD versions look great on the computer or when played via Apple TV. When you download a high-def show, you also get a standard-definition version of it to play on the iPod. (See Chapter 8 if you want to do that.)

Buy Audio Books

Some people like the sound of a good book, and iTunes has plenty to offer in its Audiobooks area. You can find verbal versions of the latest bestsellers. Prices depend on the title, but are usually cheaper than buying a hardback copy—which would be four times the size of your iPod anyway. Click any title's name and then the Buy Book button; the rest of the process works just like buying music.

If audio books are your thing, you can find even more of them—all iTunes- and iPod-friendly—at Audible.com (*www. audible.com*), a Web store devoted to selling all kinds of audio books, recorded periodicals like *The New York Times*, and radio shows. To purchase Audible's wares, though, you need to go to the site and create an Audible account. The Audible site has all the details, plus a selection of subscription plans to choose from.

If you use Windows, you'll need to download a small piece of software from Audible called Audible Download Manager, which slings your Audible files into iTunes. Mac fans don't need to worry about that, as the Audible files land directly in iTunes when you buy them.

Buy iPod Games

The iTunes Store first started selling games when the original video iPods appeared on the scene. There are now dozens of titles for sale designed to work with older video iPods as well as the iPod Classic and video-playing Nanos. (The Touch has its own outlet for games, described over there on the next page. Feel free to move on, Touch owners.)

Gaming classics like Ms. PAC-MAN, Tetris, and Sonic the Hedgehog are among the offerings. Newer titles like Spore Origins, Sudoku, Bejewled, Peggle, and several Sims games are also in stock. And there are video versions of old kitchen-table favorites like Monopoly, Uno, Scrabble, and Mah-jong.

Buying and downloading a game is just like buying anything else in the Store. Once you buy a game, it shows up in the iPod Games library in the Source list (click a purchased title to see accompanying directions). After you sync the game to your iPod, you can find it in iPod→Extras→Games. When you start the game, your iPod's scroll wheel and center button are transformed into game controls.

Unlike music or video files, however, you can play iPod games only on the iPod. They don't, alas, work in iTunes.

Buy iPod Touch Apps

One of the newest departments in the iTunes Store is the App Store. It hosts thousands of little programs you can add to your iPod Touch to make it a tiny pocket computer *and* a stylish media machine. Currency converters, 3-D video games, newsreaders, ebooks, blogging tools, guitar-chord programs, and mobile versions of popular sites like Facebook and eBay are among the many offerings.

Many apps are free (click the All Free Applications link to see them all corralled), and most cost less than $10. Click the category links on the left side of the window to browse the available software.

You purchase apps just like music and movies: see, click, buy. Your programs sync up when you connect the Touch with iTunes. (You can also buy apps right on the Touch, as Chapter 3 explains.) Some programs for sale are intended for the iPhone and its hardware, though, so as with any software: check the system requirements before you buy.

CATEGORIES

All iPhone Applications
All iPod touch Applications
All Free Applications
Books
Business
Education
Entertainment
Finance
Games
Healthcare & Fitness
Lifestyle
Music
Navigation
News
Photography
Productivity
Reference
Social Networking
Sports
Travel
Utilities
Weather

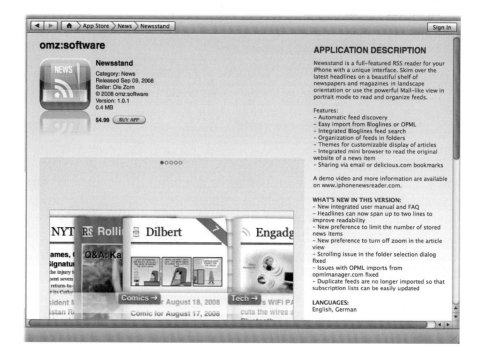

Download and Subscribe to Podcasts

The iTunes Store is host to thousands upon thousands of *podcasts,* those free audio (and video!) programs put out by everyone from big television networks to a guy in his basement with a microphone.

If you want to see what podcasts are available, click the Podcasts link on the Store's main page. You're then whisked to the Podcasts section, where you can browse shows by category, search for podcast names by keyword (use the Search iTunes Store box), or click around until you find something that sounds good.

Many podcasters produce regular installments of their shows, releasing new episodes as they're ready. You can have iTunes keep a look out for fresh editions of your favorite podcasts and automatically download them. All you have to do is *subscribe* to the podcast: click the podcast you want, and then click the Subscribe button.

If you want to try out a single podcast, click the Get Episode link near its title to download just that one show. Some attention-needy podcast producers don't give you the single-episode download option; in those cases, you'll see a Subscribe Only link near the title.

Usage Rights: What You Can Do with Your Purchases

The stuff you buy at the iTunes Store is yours to keep (unless you rented it). You're not charged a monthly fee, and your digitally protected downloads don't go *poof!* after a certain amount of time. Nor do the songs come with such confusing usage rights that you need a lawyer to figure out if you can burn a song to a CD or not. Still, you must follow a few simple rules:

- You can play downloaded songs on up to five different iTunes-equipped Macs or PCs (in any combination) and you can burn them onto CDs (seven times for each playlist).

- You can watch movies, videos, and TV shows on any five computers, on as many iPods as you own, or piped over to the TV with an AV cable or via an Apple TV box.

- A single iPod can host purchased items from up to five different accounts, but won't accept any files from a sixth account—a restriction designed to prevent a single iPod from filling up with copyrighted content purchased by, say, members of the entire sophomore class.

You can burn backup CDs and DVDs of your purchases, but you can't burn an iTunes movie or TV show to a disc and watch it on your DVD player. (On the flip side, some newer DVDs now come with an "iTunes Digital Copy" that you can add to your library from the disc; instructions are in the package.)

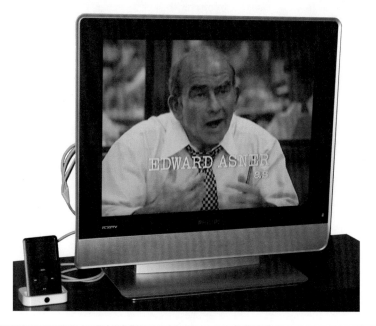

Publish Your Own Playlists (iMixes)

An *iMix* is a playlist that you publish on the iTunes Store, so everyone on earth can see your masterwork. You can name it, write your own liner notes explaining your mixing inspiration, and put it out there for everyone to see. (You're not actually copying songs up to the Store; you're just showing off your cool tastes, which Apple hopes will lead others to buy those songs.) Here's how:

❶ Start by signing into your Store account.

❷ Then, in the iTunes Source list, select the playlist you want to publish. (If it contains any songs that Apple doesn't sell, they'll get knocked off the list— which may ruin your carefully constructed mix.)

❸ Choose Store→"Create an iMix" and follow the steps on screen.

❹ Click the Publish button after you fill in all the info about your playlist.

Once you click the Publish button, your playlist is released into the wild. Now other people can see your playlist, rate it, be inspired by it, or—and let's face it, here's the main thing—buy the songs for themselves.

Other Cool iTunes Store Features

Apple's loaded the iTunes Store with plenty of unique, ear-inspiring special collections—all designed to separate you from your money. Just click the Music link on the Store's main page and head to the box titled "More in Music":

- **Best of the Store.** New music arrives on the virtual shelves regularly and the Store staff captures the zeitgeist with this weekly playlist of fresh hot tracks.

- **iTunes Essentials.** Looking for a quick course in, say, the works of Johnny Cash or Jock Rock? Usually filled to three levels, starting with well-known works and progressing to more obscure tracks, these playlists are great fun.

- **Celebrity Playlists.** See what the stars are playing on their iPods. Hundreds of actors and musicians share their personally annotated playlists—for better and for worse.

- **Nike Sport Music.** Designed for active folks who use the Nike+iPod Sport Kit, these playlists are intended to pep up your workout with a mix of hip-hop, pop, and other high-energy tracks.

- **My iTunes.** Blogs and social networking sites like Facebook give you a place on the Web to call your very own. The Store's My Tunes feature offers easy-to-use widgets and RSS code you can paste into your home on the Web. Great for letting friends know what you're listening to these days so they can admire your musical taste.

> **Tip** The iTunes U link on the main Store page leads to audio or video content from hundreds of schools around the country. Presentations, video tours, lectures, and more are all available at iTunes U—yay, rah, Fightin' Downloaders!

iTunes Gift Certificates: Buy 'Em and Spend 'Em

Gift certificates make perfect presents for people who have everything—especially when purchased by people who are lousy shoppers. These redeemable email coupons are also an excellent way to save face in potentially unpleasant situations. ("Honey, you may think that I forgot our anniversary again, but... check your email!")

Buying

To buy one, click Buy iTunes Gifts on the main page of the iTunes Store and then click the type of gift you want to send. After you choose delivery by either email or in person (you can print gift certificates yourself) the process is like buying anything on the Web: you fill in your address, gift amount, personalized message, and so on.

If you already have an Apple ID, you can log in and request to have your credit card billed; if not, sign up for one. Once you complete all the pixel paperwork, your gift certificate will be on its way.

Spending

However they arrive, iTunes Store gift certificates are meant to be spent. Here's how they work:

- If you're lucky enough to be the recipient of an iTunes email gift, redemption is just a click away. Click the Redeem link in the iTunes Store window. Copy the Redeem Code from your email and paste it into the box provided. Click Redeem. Then start shopping.

- If the gift arrived by hand (or you received an iTunes Gift Card), start up iTunes and click iTunes Store in the Source list. On the Store's main page, click the Redeem link. Type in the confirmation number printed on the gift certificate and click Redeem.

Email Gift Certificates

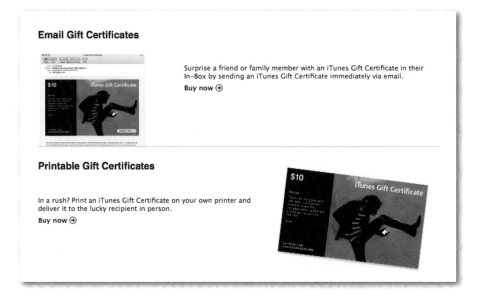

Surprise a friend or family member with an iTunes Gift Certificate in their In-Box by sending an iTunes Gift Certificate immediately via email.

Buy now ⊕

Printable Gift Certificates

In a rush? Print an iTunes Gift Certificate on your own printer and deliver it to the lucky recipient in person.

Buy now ⊕

If you already have an iTunes Store account, log in and start shopping. If you've never set your mouse pointer inside the Store before, you'll need to create an Apple Account. You have to provide your name and address, but you don't have to surrender a credit card number. If you choose None, you can use your gift certificate as the sole payment method—and end your shopping experience once you've burned through it.

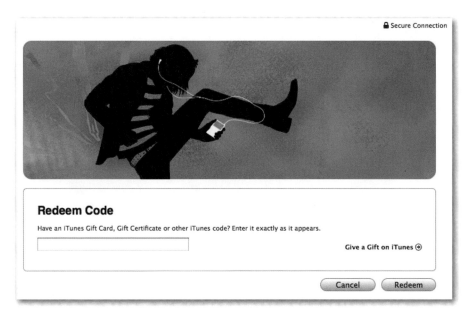

🔒 Secure Connection

Redeem Code

Have an iTunes Gift Card, Gift Certificate or other iTunes code? Enter it exactly as it appears.

Give a Gift on iTunes ⊕

(Cancel)   (Redeem)

Other Ways to Send iTunes Gifts

If you want something more personalized than an email message, you have two other options for giving someone an iTunes-themed gift.

The brightly colored prepaid iTunes Music Card is a fun spin on the gift certificate concept. Available in many different dollar amounts, givers can find cards at places like Amazon.com, Target, and Apple's own stores. You can also buy them in the iTunes Store (and have them mailed out by the Postal Service) by clicking the Buy iTunes Gifts link. Recipients can spend it all in one place—the iTunes Store—by clicking the link for Redeem on the Store's main page.

In a daring feat of bending a noun into a verb, the iTunes Store also lets you "gift" selections of music and videos to intended recipients, giving them the ability to download your thoughtful picks right from the Store onto their own computers. You can send songs, albums, and playlists to any pal with an email address, as well as audio books, music videos, and TV shows. Just look for the "Gift This..." link on the item's page.

iTunes Allowance Accounts

Allowance accounts are a lot like iTunes gift certificates. You, the parent (or other financial authority), decide how many dollars' worth of Store goods you want to give to a family member or friend (from $10 to $200). Unlike gift certificates, however, allowance accounts automatically replenish themselves on the first day of each month—an excellent way to keep music-loving kids out of your wallet while teaching them to budget their money.

Both you and the recipient need to have Apple IDs. To set up an allowance, from the iTunes Store's main page, click the Buy iTunes Gifts link, scroll down to the Allowances section and click "Set up an allowance now". Fill out the form. After you select the amount you want to deposit each month, fill in your recipient's Apple ID and password.

Once the giftee logs into the designated Apple Account, she can begin spending—no credit card required. Once the allowance amount has been spent, that's it for music until the following month. (Of course, if the recipient has a credit card on file, she can always put the difference on the card.) If you need to cancel an allowance account, click the Account link on the Store's main page to take care of the matter.

Set up an iTunes Allowance

An iTunes Allowance provides a simple way for family members and friends to buy music without giving them your credit card. Monthly allowances can be purchased in amounts from $10.00 to $200.00. Recipients must have an Apple account for use in the US store, which you can easily set up below. Allowances may be canceled at any time by visiting your Account Info page.

Your Name:	Ma
Recipient's Name:	Carmela
Monthly Allowance:	$20.00 ⬍ from $10.00 to $200.00
First Installment:	○ Don't send now, wait until the first of next month ◉ Send now, and on the first of next month
Recipient's Apple ID:	○ Create an Apple Account for recipient ◉ Use recipient's existing Apple Account
Apple ID:	ccc@hopnet.com
Verify Apple ID:	ccc@hopnet.com
Personal Message:	Don't spend it all at once! And please, honey, no bagpipe music for a while...

Cancel   Continue

Make an iTunes Wish List

With no paper money flying about to remind you of reality, it's easy to rack up hefty credit card charges. Consider, then, making an iTunes *wish list* to help keep track of songs you want to buy...when your budget is ready.

Making an iTunes wish list is basically just like making any ol' playlist, except you populate it with 30-second song previews from the iTunes Store—complete with their Buy Song buttons that take you right back to the Store once you're ready to shop again.

❶ Make a new playlist in iTunes (File→New Playlist)—"Wish List" is a good name.

❷ In the iTunes Source list, click the Store icon.

❸ Shop around the store and drag songs into the new playlist.

> **Tip** Tired of scrolling down to the bottom of iTunes to get to your wish list? (That often happens when you've loaded iTunes with playlists, which get listed alphabetically.) Slap an "@" sign at the beginning of the playlist name—*@Wish List*—and your list pops to the top of the Playlist area.

What to Do If Your Download Gets Interrupted

It's bound to happen sometime: You're breathlessly downloading a hot new album or movie from iTunes and the computer freezes, crashes, or your Internet connection goes on the fritz. Or you and your iPod Touch were in the middle of snagging an album from the iTunes Wi-Fi Music Store, and the rest of the gang decided it was time to leave the coffee shop.

If this happens to you, don't worry. Even if your computer crashes or you get knocked offline while you're downloading your purchases, iTunes is designed to pick up where it left off. Just restart the program and reconnect to the Internet.

If, for some reason, iTunes doesn't go back to whatever it was downloading before the incident, choose Store→"Check for Available Downloads" to resume your downloading business.

You can check for available purchases anytime you think you might have something waiting, like a new episode from a TV Show Season Pass. Bonus videos, electronic liner notes, and other content that was not downloaded to your iPod Touch from the Wi-Fi Music Store can be scooped up here, too.

Tip If you need help from a human at Apple you can either call (800) 275-2273 or email them. From the iTunes Store's main page, click the Support link. Your Web browser presents you with the main iTunes service and support page; click any link in the Customer Service area and then, at the bottom of the page that appears, fill out the Email Support form.

The Purchased Playlist

You can find your new songs and videos by clicking the Purchased play-list in the iTunes Source list. You can work with the Purchased playlist as though it were any other playlist. That is, even if you delete a track from it, the song itself still remains in your iTunes library. And behind the scenes, the corresponding music file stays in your My Music→iTunes→iTunes Music (Home→Music→iTunes→iTunes Music) folder.

If you're going to back up anything in your iTunes library, make it the Purchased list. After all, you paid for everything on it and if your hard drive goes south, that particular financial investment is toast. Lucky for you, iTunes 8 and later has a built-in backup tool that can archive copies of all the files you bought from the iTunes Store.

There's more information about backing up in Chapter 5, but if you're in a hurry, choose File→"Back Up to Disc". A box pops up to walk you through the process; make sure you have a stack of recordable CDs or DVDs handy.

Set Up Parental Controls for the Store

If you have children with their own Allowance Accounts, you may not want them wandering around the iTunes Store and buying just *anything*. With the Parental Controls feature, you can still give your children the freedom to spend and discover, but you can restrict the types of things they buy—without having to hover over them every time they click a Store link.

❶ In the iTunes Preferences box (Ctrl+comma/⌘-comma) click the Parental Control tab.

❷ A box unfurls with all the things you can choose to limit. For Store material, you can block songs and other items tagged with the Explicit label, restrict movie purchases to a maximum rating (G, PG, PG-13, or R), and choose the highest TV Show content rating allowable for kids (TV-Y, TV-Y7, TV-G, TV-PG, or TV-14). Games, too, are subject to age restrictions of 4+, 9+, 12+, and 17 years and older.

❸ Click the lock to password protect the settings box so the kids can't change it themselves.

You can also block certain icons from appearing in the iTunes Source list, including Podcasts, Internet Radio, Shared Music, or even the entire iTunes Store itself.

Play iTunes Purchases on Multiple Computers

Between work, home, and the family network, not everyone spends time on just one computer these days. So Apple lets you play Store purchases on up to five computers: Macs, PCs, or any combination. You just need to transfer the files and then type in your Apple user name and password on each computer to authorize it to play any songs, videos, or audio books purchased with that account. Each computer must have an Internet connection to relay the information back to Store headquarters. (And don't worry—you don't have to authorize each and every purchase; you authorize the computer once to play *all* the items bought from an account.)

You authorized your first machine when you initially signed up for an Apple Account. To authorize another computer:

❶ **On the computer you used to purchase an iTunes Store item, grab any file you've bought from iTunes.** You can drag the files right out of your iTunes window onto your desktop. You can also find all the song and video files in your iTunes Music folder: My Documents→My Music→iTunes→iTunes Music (Home→Music→iTunes→iTunes Music). Store files are easily recognizable by their *.m4p* or *.m4v* file extensions. Movies are stored in a folder called Movies; TV shows are stored in folders named after the show.

❷ **Move the file to the second computer.** Copy the file onto a CD or USB drive, email it to yourself, transfer it across the network, or use whatever method you prefer for schlepping files between machines.

❸ **Deposit the file in the iTunes Music folder on the second computer. Then, import the copied file into iTunes on the second computer.** To import the file, you can either choose File→"Add to Library" (and then select and open the file), or just drag the file right into the iTunes window.

❹ **In your iTunes list, select a transferred file and click the Play button.** iTunes asks for your Apple Account user name and password.

> **Tip** If all the iTunes Store goodies you want to copy have been synced to the iPod, you can transfer them right off the portable player to another iTunes-equipped computer. Flip ahead a couple pages to get the details.

⑤ Type your Apple ID and password, and click OK. This second computer is now authorized to play that file—and any other songs or files you bought using the same Apple Account.

Another way of authorizing a computer before you transfer anything is to choose Store→Authorize Computer.

> **Note** The copy-protection and restrictions are built into regular iTunes music tracks and videos. Songs and other content in the high-quality iTunes Plus format are "DRM-free"—that is, free of the digital-rights management software that disables regular iTunes tracks after you hit your usage limits.

Deauthorize Your Computer

Unless these are iTunes Plus tracks, you won't be able to play purchased music on a sixth computer if you try to authorize it. Apple's authorization system will see five other computers already on its list and deny your request. That's a drag, but copy protection is copy protection.

That means you have to deauthorize another computer if you want to play protected files on Number 6. To deauthorize a computer, choose Store→Deauthorize Computer, and then type in your Apple Account user name and password. The updated information zips back to Apple.

Are you thinking of putting that older computer up for sale? Before wiping the drive clean and sending it on its way, be sure to deauthorize it, so your new machine will be able to play copy-protected files. Erasing a hard drive, by itself, doesn't de-authorize a computer.

If you forget to deauthorize a machine before getting rid of it, you can still knock it off your List of Five, but you have to reauthorize every machine in your iTunes arsenal all over again. To make it so, in the iTunes Store, click the Account link. On the Apple Account Information page, click the Deauthorize All button.

Use Your iPod to Copy Purchases to Other Computers

You may love the convenience of buying music and movies from any Internet-connected Mac or PC—whether it's your regular computer or not. But what do you do if you buy Store stuff on a different computer (at work, say) and need an easy way to move it back to your main machine?

Sure, you can move the files as described a few pages earlier. But that's a hassle. If you have an iPod set to manually manage songs and playlists (page 106), though, you can just use that iPod to ferry Store purchases back to your regular computer. Both computers involved need to be authorized with the same iTunes account, but if you're just toting tunes around between your work and home PCs, that shouldn't be a problem. Here's what you do:

❶ Connect the iPod to Computer #1and load it up with the Store files you want to transfer.

❷ Eject the iPod from Computer #1 and connect it to Computer #2.

❸ In iTunes, choose File→"Transfer Purchases From iPod".

This painless transfer technique works only on Store-bought items, so you can't use it to, say, copy the player's entire library onto another computer.

> **Note** If you've purchased music at the iTunes Wi-Fi Music Store with your iPod Touch, iTunes automatically syncs the new tracks from the Touch with your computer's music library when you connect the two. If for some reason it doesn't, choose File→"Transfer Purchases from iPod".

See Your iTunes Purchase History and Get iTunes Store Help

The iTunes Store keeps track of what you buy and when you buy it. If you think your credit card was wrongly charged, or if you suspect that one of the kids knows your password and is sneaking in forbidden downloads, you can contact the Store or check your account's purchase history page to see what's been downloaded in your name.

Previous Purchases

(Previous) (Next)   Viewing Batch 1 out of 15

[1 ⬍] / [2003 ⬍]   (Jump)

Order Date	Order	Titles included in order	Total Price
⊙ 09/23/08	M1KG4FVLSB	Gift Certificate for Deborah Hall	$50.00
⊙ 09/20/08	M1KG4F80S2	Shakespeare, v1.2, Seller: Igor Zhadanov, Remote, v1.1, Seller: Apple Inc., iSSH, v2.0, Seller:...	$0.00
⊙ 09/12/08	M1KG4B4T...	NetNewsWire, v1.0.9, Seller: NewsGator Technologies, Inc.	$0.00
⊙ 09/05/08	M1KG48G3B7	The Daily Show with Jon Stewart 9/3/08, The Daily Show with Jon Stewart 9/4/08, Urbansp...	$5.97
⊙ 08/30/08	M1KG47825L	The Daily Show with Jon Stewart 8/28/08, The Daily Show with Jon Stewart 8/29/08, Three ...	$13.93
⊙ 08/26/08	M1KG46DXLH	iSSH, v1.1, Seller: Dean Beeler, BlackBook Guides, v1.0, Seller: BlackBook Media Corp., Goog...	$5.41
⊙ 08/21/08	M1KG4578JY	Love On the Inside (Deluxe Fan Edition), Mad Men, Season 1	$32.98
⊙ 08/21/08	M1KG454V7H	Sol Free Solitaire, v1.1, Seller: Smallware LLC, Cube Runner, v1.2, Seller: Andy Qua, Exposur...	$0.99
⊙ 08/05/08	M1KG4200L7	Fire Drop, v1.0, Seller: Ravi korukonda, AIM, v1.2, Seller: AOL, Apache Lander, v1.0, Seller: i...	$0.00
⊙ 07/31/08	M1KG40TZ0S	SimStapler, v1.1, Seller: Freeverse, Inc., Movies, v1.1, Seller: Jeffrey Grossman, Shakespeare,...	$0.00
⊙ 07/23/08	M1KG3Z8F9S	WeatherBug, v1.0, Seller: AWS Convergence Technologies, Inc., Urbanspoon, v1.01, Seller: ...	$0.00

(Report a Problem)   (Done)

To do the latter, on the iTunes Store's main page, click the Account link, type in your password, and then click Purchase History. Your latest purchase appears at the top of the page, and you can scroll farther down to see a list of previous acquisitions. Everything billed to your account over the months and years is here, including gift-certificate purchases. If you see something wrong, click the "Report a Problem" link and say something.

If you have other issues with your account or want to submit a specific query or comment, the online help center awaits. From the iTunes Store's main page, click the Support link. Your Web browser presents you with the main iTunes service and support page; click the link that best describes what you want to learn or complain about. For billing or credit card issues, check out the Billing Support section on that same Web page.

Note The iTunes Store sends out invoices by email, but they don't arrive right after you buy a song. You usually get an invoice that groups together all the songs you purchased within a 12-hour period, or for every $20 worth of tunes that you buy.

Buy Songs from Other Music Stores

There are many online music services out there and every one of 'em wants to sell you a song. But due to copy-protection, some of these merchants' songs don't work on the iPod. Some of them do, though. Thanks to recent moves by many stores to strip out the digital-rights management (DRM) protection on song files, their music has been liberated into the friendly MP3 play-anywhere format. Vive la musique!

Buying new songs is as easy as supplying your credit card number and downloading a file from a Web browser. Once the file is on your computer, use the File→"Add to Library" command in iTunes to add it to your collection. Here are some of the online music services that now work with the iPod:

- **Napster.** You don't get the full Napster software and services, but Windows and Mac users can download and save MP3 files to your iTunes folder through the Napster Web site. (*www.napster.com*)

- **eMusic.** Geared toward indie bands, eMusic offers several subscription plans based on quantity: 12 bucks a month, for example, gets you 30 songs of your choice to download. (*www.emusic.com*)

- **Amazon MP3 Downloads.** From the main page, click Digital Downloads and then choose MP3 Downloads. Amazon has a free piece of software called the Amazon MP3 Downloader that takes half a minute to install and automatically tosses your purchases into iTunes for you. Click the link (circled below) at the top of the Amazon MP3 page to snag the Downloader program. (*www.amazon.com*)

It's Showtime: Playing Videos

Video-playing iPods have been around since October 2005, when Apple's standard iPod arrived with a video chip inside. These days, any iPod (except for the tiny, screenless Shuffle) can handle moving pictures. But there's one that displays video especially well. With its high-resolution 3.5-inch screen, the Touch seems like it was *made* to play video, even though it does music and the Web just fine, too.

No matter which iPod you're using, you're not stuck just watching two- or three-minute music video clips, either. As explained in the previous chapter, the iTunes Store has all kinds of cinematic goodies to buy: full-length Hollywood movies and episodes (or entire seasons) of certain TV shows. Some of these are even available in the super-sharp high-definition format that looks great on the TV or computer screen. And yes, there are also thousands of music videos, just like the kind MTV used to play back when it, uh, played music.

This chapter shows you how to get all these videos from computer to iPod—and how to enjoy them on your own Shirt Pocket Cinema.

Add Videos to iTunes

The iTunes Store is chock full of videos to buy. But sometimes you've got your own flicks you want to add to iTunes. No problem. Just drag the file's icon from your desktop and drop it anywhere in iTunes' main window, or choose File→"Add to Library" to locate and import your files. Once you get videos into iTunes, you can play them in iTunes or copy them to your iPod.

Movies and TV shows have their own icons in the Source pane's Library section. Click either one to see a list of items in either category. (Music videos are lumped together in a playlist titled "Music Videos.")

If you've imported a video yourself and want it to appear in either the Movies or TV Shows section of the Source pane, you may need to tweak the file's labeling info. Open the file's Get Info box (Ctrl+I/⌘-I), click the Options tab, and then choose the video format you want from the Video Kind drop-down menu: Movie, Music Video, or TV Show.

Play Videos in iTunes

Cranking up your iTunes movie theater is a lot like playing a song: Double-click your chosen video's title and iTunes starts playing it. When you click either the Grid or Cover Flow view buttons (circled), you see the videos represented by either a movie-poster type picture or a frame from the video. (Like album covers, videos purchased from the iTunes Store come with the nice artwork.)

iTunes gives you a few video-viewing options. You can play the video in iTunes' lower-left corner artwork window, opt to have it open in a separate, floating window (as shown here), or watch it at full-screen size on your computer.

To make your screen-size choice, in the iTunes Preferences box (Ctrl+comma/⌘-comma), click the Playback tab. Make your decision using the drop-down menus for movies and TV shows, and music videos.

You can also pick a variety of screen sizes under the View→Video Size menu in iTunes, including Half Size, Actual Size, Double Size, Fit to Screen, and Full Screen.

Transfer Videos to the iPod

Chapter 1 gives you the lowdown on syncing all kinds of files between iTunes and your trusty iPod. If you don't feel like flipping back there, here's a quick summary:

- **Automatic synchronization.** Connect your iPod to the computer and click its Source pane icon in iTunes. Click the Movies tab and turn on the "Sync movies" checkbox. You can also choose to sync only certain movies to save space on your iPod. If you have TV programs in your iTunes library, click the TV Shows tab and adjust your syncing preferences there.

- **Manual management.** Click the appropriate library in the Source list (Movies or TV Shows), and then drag the files you want from the main iTunes window onto the icon of your connected iPod.

If you've made any video playlists in iTunes, you can copy those over to the iPod just like you do with music playlists. In case you haven't tried it, making a video playlist is just like making a music playlist. Chapter 6 has all the details on making and modifying iTunes playlists.

Video Formats That Work on the iPod

As described in Chapter 7, the iTunes Store now sells movies, music videos, and TV shows. You can also import into iTunes your own home movies, downloaded movie trailers, and other videos, as long as the files have one of these file extensions at the end of their name: *.mov*, *.m4v*, or *.mp4*.

Other common video formats like *.avi* or Windows Media Video (*.wmv*) won't play in iTunes, but you can convert them with Apple's $30 QuickTime Pro software or any of the dozens of video-conversion programs floating around the Web. (If you're unsure whether a file's compatible, it's always worth trying to drag it into iTunes' main window and then choosing Advanced→"Create iPod or iPhone Version".)

Here are a few popular video-conversion tools:

- **PQ DVD to iPod Video Converter Suite**. This $40 program for Windows converts TiVo recordings, DVD video, DiVX, Windows Media Video, RealMedia, and AVI files to the iPod's video format (*www.pqdvd.com*).

- **Videora iPod Converter**. With this free software, you can gather up all those *.avi* and *.mpg* video clips stashed away on your PC and turn them into iPod video clips. Find it at *www.videora.com*.

- **ViddyUp!** Mac OS X owners can convert their movies, even those in *.avi* and DiVx formats, with this $10 shareware program (*www.splasm.com*).

- **HandBrake.** Now available in versions for Windows and Mac OS X, this easy-to-use bit of freeware converts DVD movies and other files for the iPod. You can get it at *http://handbrake.fr*.

Play Videos on the Classic and Nano

Videos you buy from the iTunes Store (and other iTunes-friendly videos) appear in the iPod's Videos menu after you copy them onto the device. To watch a music video, TV show, or movie, scroll through the various Video submenus (Movies, Rentals, and so on) until you find something you want to watch.

Say you want to watch a TV Show. Select TV Shows from the main Videos menu. The next screen lists all your iPod's TV shows by title. Scroll to the show you want to watch. On the next screen, select the *episode* you want, and then press the Play/Pause button to start the show. If you have a fourth-generation Nano, turn it sideways for maximum viewing pleasure.

Here's a quick tour of the iPod's main video playback controls:

- **Press the Play/Pause button again to pause the program.** Pausing on the iPod works just like hitting Pause on a VCR or TiVo so you can get more Doritos. Press the button again to pick up where you left off.

- **To increase or decrease the video's volume, run your finger along the scroll wheel.** This volume adjustment feature works just like it does when controlling sound levels on songs.

- **To fast-forward or rewind through part of a video, tap the Select button twice.** A time code bar appears along the bottom of the screen. Use the scroll wheel to advance or retreat through a big chunk of the video. For moving forward and backward in smaller increments, hold down the Fast-Forward and Rewind buttons on the click wheel.

When your video ends, the iPod flips you back to the menu you were last on before you started watching your show. If you want to bail out before the movie's over, press the Menu button.

Some video files come in a letterbox format that leaves a strip of black screen above and below your video on the iPod. If you're not into widescreen HamsterVision, visit the Settings area of the iPod's Videos menu and change the "Fit to Screen" option to On.

Tip Want your video file to remember its position when you pause or stop it? Easy. In iTunes, select the video and then press Ctrl+I (⌘-I). Click the Options tab and turn on the checkbox next to "Remember playback position".

Play Videos on the iPod Touch

To play a video on the iPod Touch, just find the one you want in the Videos menu and tap it to start the show. But there's one thing about having an iPod with no physical control buttons: the playback controls are *on* the screen.

When you're playing video, *anything* else on the screen is distracting, so Apple hides these video playback controls. Tap the screen once to make them appear, and again to make them disappear. Here's what they do:

- **Done.** Tap this blue button, in the top-left corner, to stop playback and return to the master list of videos.

- **Scroll slider.** This progress indicator (top of the screen) is exactly like the one you see when you're playing music. You see the elapsed time, remaining time, and a little white round handle that you can drag to jump forward or back in the video.

- **Zoom/Unzoom.** In the top-right corner, a little ▧ or ▨ button appears. Tap it to adjust the zoom level of the video, as described on the facing page.

- **Play/Pause (▶/‖).** These buttons do the same thing to video as they do to music: alternate between playing and pausing.

- **Previous, Next (|◀◀, ▶▶|).** Hold down your finger to rewind or fast-forward the video. The longer you hold, the faster the zipping. (When you fast-forward, you even get to hear the sped-up audio, at least for the first few seconds.)

If you're watching a movie from the iTunes Store, you may be surprised to discover that it comes with predefined chapter markers, just like a DVD. Internally, it's divided up into scenes. You can tap the ◄◄ or ►►| button to skip to the previous or next chapter marker—a great way to navigate a long movie quickly.

- **Volume.** You can drag the round, white handle of this scroll bar (bottom of the screen) to adjust the volume.

Zoom/Unzoom

The iPod Touch's screen is bright, vibrant, and stunningly sharp. (It's got 480 by 320 pixels, crammed so tightly that there are 163 of them per inch, which is nearly twice the resolution of a computer screen.) It's not, however, the right shape for videos.

Standard TV shows are squarish, not rectangular. So when you watch TV shows, you get black letterbox columns on either side of the picture.

Movies have the opposite problem. They're *too* wide for the iPod screen. So when you watch movies, you wind up with *horizontal* letterbox bars above and below the picture.

Some people are fine with that. After all, HDTV sets have the same problem; people are used to it. At least when letterbox bars are onscreen, you know you're seeing the complete composition of the scene the director intended.

Other people can't stand letterbox bars. You're already watching on a pretty small screen; why sacrifice some of that precious area to black bars?

Fortunately, the Touch gives you a choice. If you double-tap the video as it plays, you zoom in, magnifying the image so it fills the entire screen. Or, if the playback controls are visible, you can also tap ▦ or ▦ .

Truth is, part of the image is now off the screen; now you're not seeing the entire composition as originally created. You lose the top and bottom of TV scenes, or the left and right edges of movie scenes.

Fortunately, if this effect winds up chopping off something important—some text on the screen, for example—restoring the original letterbox view is just another double-tap away.

YouTube Videos on the iPod Touch

YouTube, of course, is the stratospherically popular video-sharing Web site, where people post short videos of every type: funny clips from TV, home-made blooper reels, goofy short films, musical performances, bite-sized serial dramas, and so on. Of course, you already have a Web browser on your Touch—Safari. Why not just go to YouTube in the Web browser, the way millions of other people do?

Mainly because of Flash. Most YouTube movies are in a format called Flash, which the Touch doesn't recognize. Apple, however, convinced YouTube to re-encode all of its millions of videos into H.264, a *much* higher quality format. And one that's playable on the iPhone, iPod Touch, and Apple TV.

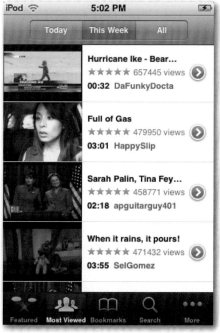

Finding a Video to Play

The YouTube program works much like the iPod's Music and Videos menus; it's basically a collection of lists. Tap one of the icons at the bottom of the screen, for example, to find videos in any of these ways:

- **Featured.** A scrolling, flickable list of videos hand-picked by YouTube's editors. You get to see the name, length, star rating, and popularity (viewership) of each one.

- **Most Viewed.** A popularity contest. Tap the buttons at the top to look over the most-viewed videos *Today*, *This Week*, or *All* (meaning "of all time"). Scroll to the bottom of the list and tap Load 25 More to see the next chunk of the list.

- **Bookmarks.** A list of videos you've flagged as your own personal faves, as described in a moment.

- **Search.** Makes the Touch's keyboard appear, so you can type a search phrase. YouTube produces a list of videos whose titles, descriptions, keywords, or creator names match what you typed.

If you tap More, you get three additional options:

- **Most Recent.** These are the very latest videos that have been posted on YouTube.

- **Top Rated.** Whenever people watch a video on YouTube, they have the option of giving it a star rating. (You can't rate videos when you're viewing them on the Touch.) This list rounds up the highest rated videos. Beware—you may be disappointed in the taste of the masses.

- **History.** This is a list of videos you've viewed recently on the Touch—and a Clear button that nukes the list, so that people won't know you've been watching that "Charlie Bit My Finger" video.

Each of these lists offers a ⊙ button at the right side. Tap it to open the Details screen for that video, featuring a description, date, category, tags (keywords), uploader name, play length, number of views, links to related videos, etc.

Also on this screen is the button which adds this video to your own personal list of favorites. Tap the Bookmarks button at the bottom of the screen to see that list.

Playing YouTube Videos

To play a video, tap its row in any of the lists. Turn the Touch 90 degrees counter-clockwise—all videos play in horizontal orientation. The video begins playing automatically; you don't have to tap the ▶ button.

When you first start playing a video, you get the usual iPod controls, like ▶▶|, |◀◀, ||, the volume slider, and the progress scrubber which lets you move to a different spot in the video. Here again, you can double-tap the screen to magnify the video, just enough to eliminate the black bars on the sides of the screen (or tap the ⬚ button at the top-right corner to do the same).

The controls fade away after a moment, so they don't block your view. You can make them appear and disappear with a single tap on the video.

Finally, there are two other icons on these controls: The first is the ⊓ button, which adds the video you're watching to your Bookmarks list, so you won't have to hunt around for it later. The second is the ✉ button, which lets you share your discovery by e-mail. A quick tap attaches a YouTube link to a fresh message in Touch Mail.

Finally, there's a Done button at the top-left corner. It takes you out of the video you're watching and back to the list of YouTube videos.

Play iTunes and iPod Videos on Your TV

Movies on the iPod and computer screen are great, but watching them on a bigger screen is often even more gratifying. In case you were wondering, you *can* watch all those movies and videos on your big TV screen—you just need to connect your computer or iPod to the television. *What* you connect them with depends on the hardware involved.

If you're connecting the computer to the TV, here are your best options:

- Connect computers that have S-video connections using an S-video cable; that pipes through high-quality video. For the audio, a $10 Y-shaped cable with a stereo mini-plug on one end and the red and white RCA plugs on the other provide the sound.

- If you have a computer-friendly television (the kind that can double as a computer monitor thanks to VGA or DVI ports), you can just plug your laptop right into the TV.

To mate the iPod with the TV, your options depend on which generation iPod you have.

- **Early video iPods, (the ones that came out before Apple dubbed the model the "Classic").** You can connect these iPods to the TV with a

> **Tip** Not sure which iPod you have? Apple has a handy illustrated chart of every Pod that ever scrolled the Earth at *http://support.apple.com/kb/HT1353*. And if you're not sure which ones support TV Out, see *http://support.apple.com/kb/HT1454*.

special cable like the Apple iPod AV Cable, available at *http://store.apple. com* and other places. This $19 cable has a stereo mini-plug on one end for the iPod's headphones jack, and red, white, and yellow RCA plugs on the other end for carrying the audio and video signal to the TV. Some similar camcorder cables may also work, as do third-party cables from Belkin and Monster Cable, or special iPod video docks from DLO and other companies.

- **The iPod Classic, video Nano, or iPod Touch.** You, new iPod owner, need a different cable—one that can unlock the iPod's ability to pipe video to the TV screen. (Older iPod cables and many third-party offerings won't work with these models, unless you're using them with one of Apple's Universal Docks for iPods.)

The easiest place to find these cables is the Apple Store (*http://store. apple.com*). Here, you can find the Apple Composite AV Cable for TVs with the older video inputs. You can also find the Apple Component AV Cable, made for high-end TVs and widescreen sets that can use the higher-quality component connection. Both versions of the Apple cable cost about $50, but you do get an integrated AC adapter on there to make sure your 'Pod is powered for the whole weekend movie marathon.

Several third-party companies also make video docks and cables for the iPod; see Chapter 12 to get an idea of who's selling what. If you do go with a non-Apple product, make sure it's rated to work with your particular iPod make and model.

Settings	
TV Out	On
TV Signal	NTSC
TV Screen	Widescreen
Fit to Screen	Off
Alternate Audio	Off
Captions	Off
Subtitles	Off

Once you connect your iPod to the television set, tweak it so the video picture appears on the big screen: choose iPod→Videos→Settings and set TV Out to "On". (The TV Out settings on the iPod Touch are at Home→Settings→Video.)

The other Settings options are pretty self-explanatory. (The exception: TV Signal. Choose NTSC if you live in the U.S. or Japan, or pick PAL if you're connecting to a European or Australian TV set).

Once you get the iPod or computer hooked up to play movies, be sure to select the alternate video source on your television set, just as you would to play a DVD or game.

Back Up Your Video Collection to DVD

Don't get too excited: You can burn your iTunes Store movies, music videos, TV shows, and other itty bitty videos to a recordable DVD, but you can't actually *play* that disc in your living room DVD player. The DVD burning you do here is only for backing up your files.

Some movie download services like Movielink and CinemaNow let customers buy a download and burn that file to a playable DVD (which is a lot more convenient than schlepping out to Blockbuster on a dark and stormy night). Maybe the iTunes Store will allow that down the road, but for now, it's Backup Only.

If you don't remember the steps from Chapter 5 explaining how to back up your files to a disc, here's the highlight reel:

❶ In iTunes, select the video playlist you want to back up (or just jump to Step 2 and back up your whole Purchased playlist or entire iTunes library).

❷ Choose File→"Back Up to Disc".

❸ Feed your computer as many recordable or rewritable DVDs as it wants during the process.

When iTunes is done, store the discs in a safe place.

Closed Captioning on Videos

Some videos now include *closed captioning*—short text descriptions of a scene's action and dialogue, displayed on the screen for people who have impaired hearing. If you have closed-captioned video files in your iTunes library, you can turn on the text both on your computer and on your iPod.

To set it up in iTunes, open the Preferences box (Ctrl+comma/⌘-comma), click the Playback tab, and then put a check in the box next to "Show closed captioning when available".

If you have video files with embedded subtitles or alternative audio tracks, you can set your preferences for those here as well. If you need to adjust any settings while playing a video, choose Control→"Audio & Subtitles in iTunes" and select the language option or whatever you need. (This menu is grayed out unless you actually have a video with subtitles or alternative audio.)

The iPod has its own settings to display closed captions as well:

- On the Classic or Nano, choose iPod→Videos→Settings→Captions and click the iPod's center button to toggle them On or Off.

- On the iPod Touch, tap your way to Home→Settings→Video to get to the Closed Captioning controls.

Tip If you're having trouble finding movies that have closed captioning, let iTunes do the looking. On the main page of the iTunes Store, click the Power Search link, choose Movies, and turn on the checkbox next to "Search for movies that contain closed captioning" before you click the Search button.

Picturing Your Photos on the iPod

Who needs an overstuffed wallet with cracked plastic picture sleeves to show off your snaps? If you have an iPod Classic, Nano, or Touch, you can quickly dump all your favorite shots right onto the iPod and view them on the glossy color screen. The picture-perfect fun doesn't stop there, either. Like earlier versions of the iPod and Nano, this trio of iPods can also display your photos in mini-slideshow form, right in the palm of your hand. And with most modern iPods, you can plug them into the television set with a special AV cable and fire up those slideshows on the living-room screen. This chapter shows you how to do everything except microwave the popcorn for the big show.

Setting Up: Get Ready to Put Photos on the iPod

In addition to a computer loaded with iTunes and an iPod with a color screen, you need a few other things to move pictures to 'Pod:

- **Compatible photo software for the Mac or Windows—or a folder of photos on your hard drive.** iPods can sync with several popular photo programs that you may already have. On the Mac, there's Aperture or iPhoto 6 or later. Windows mavens can grab pictures from Adobe Photoshop Album or the more versatile Adobe Photoshop Elements. You can also transfer pictures from a folder of photos on your computer, like the iPhoto Library folder for those who are a few iPhoto versions behind, or My Pictures on the Windows side of the fence.

- **Digital photographs in the proper format.** Most of the common photo formats used by digital cameras, Web pages, and email programs are acceptable to iTunes, along with a few others. On the Mac, you can use JPG and GIF files, as well as images in the PICT, TIFF, BMP, PNG, JPG2000, SGI, and PSD formats. In Windows, JPG, GIF, TIF, BMP, PSD, SGI, and PNG files work for the iPod.

You should remember a few other things when adding images to your iPod. For one, you can't import pictures off one of those photo CDs from the drugstore or a backup disc you made yourself—iTunes needs to pull the photos directly from your hard drive. Photos stored on DVDs or CDs won't cut it, either. (In other words, you need to first transfer the pix from disk to computer, and **then** they're ready for your iPod.)

The iPod allies itself with one computer when it comes to photos. Unlike manual music management, where you can grab songs from several different computers, synchronizing pictures can happen only between one iPod and one computer. If you want to load photos from a different computer, all the photos currently on the iPod will be replaced with ones from the new machine.

You also can't dump photos directly into the iPod from your digital camera— you need to go through iTunes, unless you have a much older iPod and a gadget like the iPod Camera Connector (available for $29 at *http://store.apple. com*) that can siphon photos from the camera's memory card over to the iPod's hard drive. These devices don't work with the iPod Nano, though, nor do they work on the iPod Classic or Touch.

Get Pictures onto the iPod

Okay, so you've got the right iPod and a bunch of pictures in iTunes-friendly formats on your hard drive. How do those photos get from your hard drive to the iPod? They get there like the music does—through iTunes.

But first, you need to set up your iTunes and iPod preferences to copy the photos you want to carry around, like so:

❶ Connect the iPod to your Mac or PC with its USB cable.

❷ Once the iPod shows up in the iTunes Source list, click its icon to select it.

❸ In the middle of iTunes, click the iPod's Photos tab.

❹ Turn on the checkbox next to "Sync photos from" and then choose your photo program or folder of choice; that lets iTunes knows where to look for your photos. You can choose to copy over everything or just selected *albums* (sets of pictures).

❺ Click Sync (or Apply, if this is the first time) when you've made your selections.

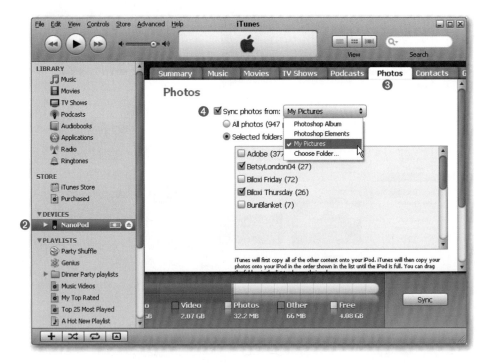

If you don't use any of the programs listed in the "Sync photos from" menu, and just want to copy over a folder of photos on your hard drive, select "Choose folder" from the pop-up menu and then navigate to the desired folder. You can sync just the photos in your chosen folder, or include the photos tucked away in folders *inside* your chosen folder, too.

Select the "All photos and albums" option if you want every single image in your photo program's library to get hauled over to the iPod. (If you don't want those bachelorette-party snaps to get copied, opt for "Selected albums" and choose only the collections you want from your photo program.)

If you choose all photos and have a small iPod, iTunes starts copying pictures in the order they appear in their albums until the iPod's full. If you're tight for space and want to make sure certain albums make it, drag the desired albums up and down the list in the iTunes window to reorder them.

Whenever you connect the iPod, it syncs the photo groups you've designated and also picks up any new pictures you've added to these groups since you last connected. During the process, iTunes displays an "Optimizing photos..." message.

Don't let the term "optimizing" scare you: iTunes hasn't taken it upon itself to touch up your photographic efforts. The program is simply creating versions of your pictures that look good on anything from your tiny iPod screen to your TV screen (in case you end up connecting your iPod to it). Then it tucks away these copies on your hard drive before adding them to the iPod.

Once you have some pictures on your Classic or Nano, the iPod will randomly select some of the images and make a gently floating slideshow of its own on the right side or bottom of the screen when you have the Photos menu selected.

> **Tip** Want to take a snap of some cool thing on the screen of your iPod Touch? Hold down the Home button and press the Sleep/Wake button like a camera shutter. The screenshot lands in Photos→Saved Photos and can be transferred back to the computer the next time you sync. In fact, if you have a program on your computer that senses when you've connected a digital camera, it will likely leap up and offer to pull in the Touch's screenshots just like regular photos.

Digital Photographer Alert: Storing Full-Quality Photos on the iPod

When iTunes optimizes your photos for iPoddification, it streamlines the images a bit instead of copying the big, full-resolution files. But if you want, you can copy the full-size photo files. That way you can transfer them to another computer—good news if you're a photographer and want to haul around a big, print-ready photo collection.

Just follow these steps:

❶ Connect the iPod Nano or Classic and select it in the iTunes Source list. Make sure you've set up the iPod as a portable hard drive. (See Chapter 10 for details.) The short version: in your iPod's settings page in iTunes, click the Summary tab and then turn on the "Enable disk use" checkbox.

❷ Click the Photos tab in the iTunes window.

❸ Turn on the "Include full-resolution photos" checkbox.

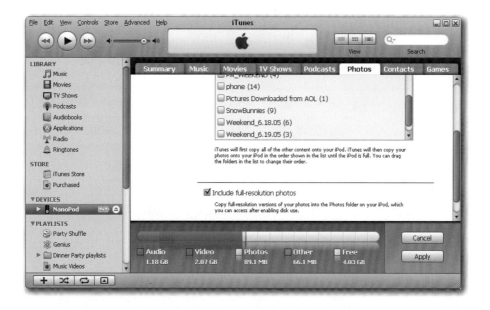

After you sync, full-resolution copies of the photos sit happily in the Photos folder on the iPod's hard drive. (The Photos folder also has a subfolder called Thumbs that's full of iPod-optimized images all scrunched up in special *.ithmb* files; you can safely ignore these.)

View Photos on the iPod Classic or Nano

Once you've got those photos freed from the confines of your computer, you'll probably want to show them off to your pals. To get to the goods, choose Photos→All Photos from the iPod's main screen. Or, if you opted for individual photo albums when setting up your synchronization preferences, scroll to the album you want to view and then press the round center button.

The iPod pops up a screen filled with tiny versions of the pictures in the group you just selected. Use the scroll wheel to maneuver the little yellow highlight box, and then zoom along the rows until you get to the picture you want to see. If you have hundreds of pee-wee pix to plow through, tap the Previous and Next buttons to advance or retreat by the screenful.

Here are some other navigational tips:

- Highlight the photo and press the center button to call up a larger version that fills the iPod screen.

- Press the Previous and Next buttons—or scroll the click wheel in either direction—to move forward or backward through pictures in an album.

- If you have a Nano, tilt it sideways to better see photos in landscape view.

- Press the Menu button to go back to the screen of tiny photos.

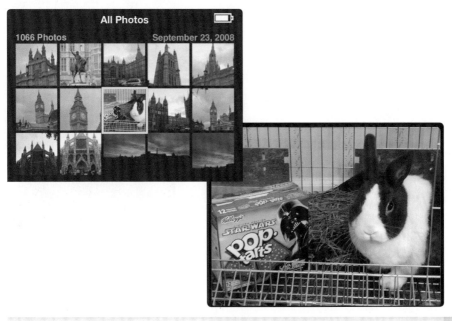

View Photos (in a Pinch) on Your iPod Touch

With its big color screen, the iPod Touch shows off your photos better than other iPods—and lets you have more fun viewing them because it's literally a hands-on experience.

To see the pictures you synced from your computer, tap the Photos icon on the iPod Touch's Home screen. Then tap Photo Library to see all your pictures in thumbnail view. If you chose to copy over specific photo albums, tap the name of the album you want to look at. To get back, tap the Photo Albums button at the top of the screen.

To see a full-screen version of a picture, tap the thumbnail image of it. The Touch's photo controls are visible for a few seconds, but you can tap the photo to make them go away. Double-tap the photo on the screen to magnify it. You can also rotate the Touch to have horizontal photos fill the width of the screen.

Here are some other things you can do with your photos on the iPod Touch:

❶ Tap the left and right arrow keys to move through the photos in the collection.

❷ Tap the triangle icon at the bottom of the screen to start a slideshow (flip to the next page to learn about slideshow settings).

❸ To set a photo as the wallpaper for your iPod Touch (you know, that background picture you see on screen when you wake the Touch from a nap), tap the swooping arrow icon in the left corner. Then tap the Use As Wallpaper button.

❹ Spread and pinch your fingers on screen (those fancy Touch moves described in Chapter 3) to zoom in and out of a photo. Drag your finger around onscreen to pan through the photo once you've zoomed in.

❺ Flick your finger horizontally across the screen in either direction to scroll through the pictures at whizzy speeds. You can show off your vacation photos *really* fast this way.

If you're using Mail on the Touch (Chapter 3), you can also email a pic to a pal. Tap the desired image to make the controls appear, then tap the 🖅 icon and select Email Photo. This attaches the picture to an outgoing message. Address it, type a note if you like, and tap the Send button.

> **Tip** Want to use a certain photo for your Touch wallpaper, but wish there wasn't that guy making faces in the background? You can crop in on photos with the ol' spread, pinch, and drag moves to suit yourself. Once you like what you see, tap the icon in the bottom-left corner and then choose the Use As Wallpaper option.

Play Slideshows on the iPod

A photo slideshow takes all the click-and-tap work out of your hands and frees you to admire the pictures without distraction. To run a slideshow on the iPod itself, you need to set up a few things, like how long each photo displays and what music accompanies your trip to Disneyland.

Settings	
Time Per Slide	>
Music	
Repeat	Off
Shuffle Photos	Off
Transitions	
TV Out	Off
TV Signal	NTSC

Slideshow Settings on a Classic or Nano

Start by choosing Photos→Settings. You'll see a slew of options to shape your slideshow experience.

- Use the Time Per Slide menu to set the amount of time each photo is displayed on screen, from 2 to 20 seconds. You can also choose to move to each new image manually with a tap of the click wheel.

- Use the Music menu to pick one of your iPod's playlists to serve as a soundtrack for your slideshow, if you want one. You may even want to compose a playlist in iTunes just to use with a particular slideshow. Mac owners: If you've already got music assigned to the photo album in iPhoto, choose the From iPhoto option at the top of the menu.

- As with your music, you can repeat and shuffle the order of your photos. You can also add fancy Hollywood-style scene transitions by choosing Photos→Settings→Transitions. Pick from several dramatic photo-changing styles, including "Zoom" and "Fade Through Black".

- To make sure the slideshow appears on the iPod's screen, set the TV Out setting to Off, which keeps the signal in the iPod. (Turn the page if you want to project this slideshow on the TV.) Or you can select Ask, so that each time you start a slideshow, the iPod inquires whether you intend to run your photos on the big or small screen.

Once you've got your settings just the way you want them, select the album or photo you want to start with, and then press the Play/Pause button on the click wheel to start the show. Press the Play/Pause button again to temporarily stop the show; press it again to continue.

Your choice of music, transitions, and time per slide all match what you chose in the Slideshow settings. If you get impatient, you can also use the Previous and Next buttons on the click wheel to manually move things along.

Slideshow Settings on an iPod Touch

To customize the way your photos slide by on your Touch screen, press the Home button on your iPod and the tap Settings→Photos. Your options include:

- **How long each picture appears on screen.** Tap the time shown to get a menu of other choices.

- **The transition effect between photos.** Dissolves, wipes, and all the usual styles are here.

You can also choose to repeat or shuffle photos in your show by tapping the Off or On buttons in the Settings area. Now, press the Home button and go back to Photos to start the show.

Note The iPod Touch doesn't include a slideshow music option in its settings. To get a soundtrack going for Touch Theater, hit the Home button, tap the Music icon and tap up a song or playlist. When the music starts, jump back to Photos and start the show from the album you want to see.

Play Slideshows on a TV

Flip back to the previous chapter if you need help connecting your iPod to the television set so you can view your digital goodies on the TV.

Note As explained in the last chapter, the type of iPod you have will dictate what equipment you need to display photos and videos on your TV. First-generation video iPods that came out between 2005 and 2006 can use the older iPod AV cable that connects through the headphone port or Line Out jack on an iPod dock. Newer Classics, Nanos, and Touches require connection through the Apple Universal Dock, the Apple Composite AV Cable, the Apple Component AV Cable, or a compatible third-party offering. In any case, it's going to cost a few bucks.

Once you've made the iPod-TV link, you're almost ready to start the show. You just need to adjust a few more things on the iPod.

For Classics, Nanos, and Older Video iPods:

❶ **Choose Photos→Settings→TV Out→On.** The On option tells the iPod to send the slideshow *out* to the TV screen instead of playing it on its own screen. (You can also set it to Ask, if you want the iPod to pester you about what screen to use.) If you're using a Classic or Nano with one of Apple's AV cables, TV Out magically works for you.

❷ **Select your local television broadcast standard.** If you're in North America or Japan, choose Photos→Settings→TV Signal→NTSC. If you're in Europe or Australia, choose Photos→Settings→TV Signal→PAL. If you're in an area not listed above, check your television's manual to see what standard it uses or search the Web for "world television standards."

❸ **Turn on your TV and select the video input source for the iPod.** You select the input for the iPod's signal the same way you tell your TV to show the signal from the DVD player or VCR. Typically, you press the Input or Display button on your TV's remote to change from the live TV signal to the new video source.

Now, cue up a slideshow on the iPod and press the Play/Pause button. Your glorious photographs—scored to the sounds of your selected music, if you wish—appear on your television screen. (Because television screens are horizontal displays, vertical shots end up with black bars along the sides.)

Your pre-selected slideshow settings control the show, or you can advance it manually with your thumb on the click wheel. If you have the iPod Universal Dock, you can also pop through shots with a click of its tiny white Apple remote control. Although just one photo at a time appears on the TV screen, if you're driving the iPod Classic, your iPod shows not only the current picture, but the one before it and the one after, letting you narrate your show with professional smoothness: "OK, this is Shalimar *before* we had to get her fur shaved off after the syrup incident…"

For the iPod Touch:

❶ **Tap Settings→Video.** When you connect an AV cable, the picture appears on the TV instead of the iPod. In the TV Out section here, you can toggle Widescreen On or Off.

❷ **In the TV Signal area, select your local television broadcast standard.** If you're in North America or Japan, choose NTSC. If you're in Europe or Australia, choose PAL.

❸ **Turn on your TV and select the video input source for the Touch.** You select the input for the iPod's signal the same way you tell your TV to show the signal from the DVD player or VCR. Typically, you press the Input or Display button on your TV's remote to change from the live TV signal to the new video source.

❹ **On the Touch, navigate to the video you want.** Press the Play triangle at the bottom of the screen. The show begins.

The iPod as Personal Assistant

The early chapters in this book are all about showing how your iPod works and how to fill it up with music, movies, photos, and more. But if you think that's *all* the iPod can do, think again. That gorgeous color screen is happy to display a copy of your computer's address book and calendar. If you're looking for a handsome timepiece, the iPod can function as a world clock when you're on the road and as a stopwatch when you're on the track.

If you've got a Nano, a Shuffle, or a Classic iPod, you can easily use it as an external hard drive for hauling around monster files like PowerPoint presentations or quarterly reports between computers. So if you've mastered the iPod's AV Club talents and are ready for new challenges, this chapter shows you even more ways to use your iPod.

iPod as an Address Book

Putting a copy of your contacts file—also known as your computer's address book—onto your iPod is quite easy, as long as you're using recent software. Windows people need to have their contacts stored in Outlook Express, Outlook 2003 (or later), Windows Contacts, or the Windows Address Book (used by Outlook Express and some other email programs).

Mac folks need to be using at least Mac OS X 10.4 (Tiger) and the Mac OS X Address Book (shown here), which Apple's Mail program uses to stash addresses in. You can also use Entourage 2004 or later, but you first have to link before you sync: in Entourage, choose Preferences and click Sync Services: then turn on the checkboxes for sharing contacts (and calendars) with Address Book and iCal (Apple's calendar program). Entourage shares the info and Address Book and iCal sync it up.

To turn your iPod into your little black book, follow these steps:

❶ Connect the iPod to the computer and click its icon when it shows up in the Source list. (Launch Outlook/Outlook Express if you use either of these.)

❷ In the main part of the iTunes window, click the Contacts tab on a Classic or Nano; go for the Info tab on the Touch.

❸ Windows owners: Turn on the checkbox next to "Sync contacts from" and then use the drop-down menu to choose the program you want to copy contacts from. Mac owners: turn on the "Sync Address Book contacts" checkbox. If you've created any contact groups, select them from the "Selected groups" box. You can also choose to import the photos in your contacts files.

❹ Click the Apply button in the lower-right corner of the iTunes window.

The iPod updates itself with the contact information stored in your address book. If you add new contacts while the iPod is plugged in, choose File→Update iPod, or click the Sync button in iTunes to manually move the new data over to your pocket player. When you decide someone doesn't deserve to be in your contacts anymore and you delete them from your computer's address book, the person will disappear from your iPod the next time you sync it to the computer.

To look up a pal on the iPod Nano or Classic, choose iPod→Extras→Contacts and scroll to the name of the person you want to look up. Press the center button and the address card for that person pops up on screen. Touch owners: tap the Contacts icon on the Home screen and flick your way to whichever contact you're looking for. Tap the name to see the details.

> **Tip** The iPod Touch has some extra features on iTunes' Info tab. First, you have the option to sync up with contacts stored in both Google Gmail and Yahoo! Address Book. Click the Configure button to enter your Gmail or Yahoo user name and password. Yes, you need an Internet connection to sync. Second, because you can enter contacts directly on the Touch, the Info settings give you the option to say which group you'd like to add your Touch-created contacts to when you return home.

iPod as a Calendar

Just as iTunes can pluck contacts off your computer, it can also snag and display a copy of your daily or monthly schedule on your iPod—*if* you happen to use Outlook on your PC, or iCal on your Mac. (You can use Entourage 2004 or later by choosing, in Entourage, Preferences→Sync Services and checking off the option for Entourage to share its event info with iCal.)

To get your calendar connected, fire up iTunes and then:

❶ Connect the iPod to your computer and click the iPod's icon when it shows up in the Source list.

❷ In the main part of the iTunes window, click the Contacts tab (or the Info tab it you have a Touch). Scroll down past Contacts to Calendars.

❸ Turn on the checkbox next to "Sync calendars from Microsoft Outlook" (Windows) or "Sync iCal calendars" (Mac). If you have multiple calendars, select the ones you want to copy to the 'Pod.

❹ In the lower-right corner of the iTunes window, click the Apply button.

❺ If the iPod doesn't automatically start updating itself with your date book, choose File→Sync iPod. If you haven't changed any settings but are just updating info, the Apply button in the corner of iTunes turns to Sync, and you can click that instead of going up to Menuville.

To look up your busy schedule on the iPod Classic or Nano, choose iPod→Extras→Calendars. Select the name of the calendar you want to examine and press the round center button. The skinny Nano screen gives you a calendar grid with dots on days with stuff scheduled and the names of events listed below. On the Classic, you get a blue and gray grid with tiny red flags planted on the squares when you have something scheduled for that day. In both models, use the scroll wheel to navigate to a particular day and press the center button to see details on the day's events.

On the iPod Touch, tap the Calendar icon on the Home screen. Tap List, Day, or Month to see your schedule in the short or long term, or tap the Today button to see what's immediately in your future. List view shows a scroll of all your upcoming appointments. In Month view, events are represented by black dots and are listed below the calendar grid. Tap the black triangles on either side of the month name to advance forward or backward through the months. Tap the + button to add an event.

A few other calendar-keeping tips:

- If you make use of the To Do list function in your calendar program, those action items appear in their own place on the Classic and Nano. Choose iPod→Extras→Calendars→To Do.

- The iPod can also pester you when you have a pending appointment that's been marked (on your PC) to pop up a reminder. To turn on the portable Nag Alerts, choose iPod→Extras→Calendars→Alarms. You have your choice of Off, Beep, or None (which just displays a silent message onscreen). The Touch will flash you a beeping on screen alert, keyed to the event reminders in your calendar program. You can also set your own alert by selecting an event and tapping the Edit button. Tap the Alert screen and pick a suitable amount time for an advance warning message.

Track Time: iPod as a Stopwatch

The iPod Nano, Classic, and Touch all have a Stopwatch feature riding alongside all their great music and video capabilities. Using the iPod stopwatch is not unlike using a regular stopwatch, except that it can be a very expensive timer. As with most things, the Touch does things its own touchy-feely way.

iPod Touch

To get to the Touch's stylish full-screen stopwatch, tap your way through Home→Clock→Stopwatch. To start timing yourself, tap the green Start button. The timer starts counting and Start changes to a red Stop button. (Tap that when you're done timing.) Or, if you're running a series of laps, tap the gray Lap button each time you finish one. The iPod Touch records your time for that Lap and then starts timing your next one.

Your lap times are displayed on screen in a list under the timer, so you can track your session. The timer keeps ticking, even if you tap your way into another program, say, to pick another playlist. When you tap the Clock icon again on the Home screen, you return to the Stopwatch, still ticking away.

If you need to pause the timer, tap the Stop button and then tap Start again to have it pick up where it left off counting. When you're finally done with your exercise, tap the Stop button to halt the clock. Then hit the gray Reset button to clear the times from the screen.

> **Tip**: The latest version of the iPod Touch has the Nike + iPod software built right in. All you have to do is tap Home→Settings→Nike + iPod to turn it on. You still need to buy the special Nike shoes and shoe sensor that transmits your steps to the iPod. Nanos need the snap-on reciever ($30 for the kit at *http://www.apple.com/ipod/nike*), but once enabled, the iPod keeps track of your workout more scientifically than any personal trainer ever could *and* you get to play your own music.

iPod Classic and Nano

The Stopwatch feature on these two iPods not only clocks your time around the track, it also *keeps* track of your running sessions. To turn your Classic or Nano into a timer, choose Extras→Stopwatch. Here's what you do from there:

- Press the Play/Pause button to begin. The iPod begins to clock you by hours, minutes, seconds, and milliseconds.

- If you're timing each lap around the track, tap the iPod's center button to record that lap time; it's then listed underneath the overall session time. The screen displays up to three lap times.

- Press Play/Pause to stop the clock. When you're done timing, press the Menu button. This takes you back to the Stopwatch menu. Here, you can click on Resume to start up the clock again.

- If you want a new session with the Stopwatch, select New Timer.

The iPod stores logs of your last several workout sessions. To review your progress, scroll to Extras→Stopwatch, where there's a list of your past exercise sessions listed by date and time of day recorded. Scroll and select a session to see a list of your lap times, with the shortest, longest, and average lap noted on top. Press the iPod's center button to delete the log.

- If you have a lot of old logs cluttering up the screen, select Extras→Stopwatch→Clear Logs to wipe them all out.

- If you're in the middle of a session, go to Extras→Stopwatch→Current Log to see your current state of progress.

Stopwatch Log	
Sep 25 2008	**6:30 AM**
Total	**00:17:05.8**
Shortest	**00:02:57.1**
Longest	**00:05:01.2**
Average	**00:04:16.4**
Lap 1	00:04:32.2
Lap 2	00:05:01.2
Lap 3	00:02:57.1
Lap 4	00:04:35.0

Tip Attention all cooks. The Touch's Timer is great for keeping track of that bubbling bouillabaisse. Nestled right next to the Stopwatch, the Timer works just as you'd expect: pick your countdown time using the virtual spinwheels and press Start.

Tick-Tock: iPod as a World Clock

As discussed earlier in this book, all iPods (except for the screenless Shuffle) have built-in clocks with a simple alarm feature. But that's *so* last week. These power Pods let you set multiple clocks, in different time zones, each with their own alarms. If you travel frequently, you can simply create a clock for each location instead of constantly fiddling with time zone settings. Cool.

The iPod should already have one clock—the one you created when you first set it up and selected your time zone.

Add a Clock on Your iPod Touch

❶ Tap Home→Clock→World Clock.

❷ Tap the plus (**+**) button in the right corner of the screen.

❸ When the keyboard pops up, start typing the name of any large city.

❹ Tap the name of the city to add its clock to your list.

If you want to rearrange your list of clocks, tap the Edit button and use the three-stripe gripstrip (≡) to drag them into the order you want.

To delete a clock, tap the Edit button. Tap the ⊖ icon next to the clock's name and then tap the Delete button to whack that clock from the list.

Add a Clock on Your iPod Classic or Nano

❶ Go to iPod→Extras→Clocks and tap the iPod's center button.

❷ You have one clock there. Click the center button again to choose Add. (Choose Edit if you just want one clock, but want to change it.)

❸ On the next screen, select a world region, like North America, Europe, Africa, or Asia. Some categories on the Region menu are less obvious: Select Atlantic if you live in Iceland or the Azores; choose Pacific if you live in Hawaii, Guam, or Pago Pago.

❹ After you select a region, the next screen takes you to a list of major cities and the current time in that part of the world. Scroll and select the city of your choice. Once you pick a city, the iPod creates a clock showing the local time and adds it to your Clock menu.

If you want to change a clock, select it and press the iPod's center button to bring up the onscreen options for Edit and Delete. Choose Edit, which takes you back through the whole "pick a region, pick a city" exercise.

If you decide you have too many clocks and don't need that Tora Bora clock after all, select the unwanted clock from the list. Press the center button on the iPod, scroll down to Delete, and press the center button again to erase time.

> **Note** To make adjustments, like changing to Daylight Saving Time or to change the iPod's current time zone, choose iPod→Settings→Date & Time on a Classic or Nano. On the Touch, hit the Home screen and then tap Settings→General→Date & Time to get to the time controls.

iPod as a Portable Hard Drive

If being a portable entertainment system and organizer isn't enough, your iPod can also serve as a portable disk to shuttle documents, presentations, and other files from one computer to another. (The Touch doesn't naturally work as an external drive unless you use utility programs like TouchCopy, which was mentioned back in Chapter 5.)

To give your iPod these file-toting powers:

❶ Plug your Pod into the computer.

❷ When the iPod icon shows up in the Source list, select it and then click the Summary tab in the main iTunes window.

❸ Turn on the checkbox next to "Enable disk use" in the Options area of the Summary screen. (If you have an iPod Shuffle, use the onscreen slide to designate just how much of your one or two gigabytes you want to use for music and how much for files.)

❹ In the lower-right corner of the iTunes window, click the Apply button. If you forget, iTunes reminds you that you modified an iPod setting and prompts you to OK the change.

Your iPod now shows up in the My Computer area of Windows or on the Mac desktop. You can drag files on and off the iPod just like you would with any other drive connected to the computer: Drag files onto the iPod's

icon, or double-click the icon and create folders to put your files in. Delete files by dragging them to the Trash or Recycle Bin. Steer clear of the folders labelled Calendars, Contacts, and Photos; the iPod uses them for storage of those items. The next page shows you how to use the Notes folder.

Keep in mind that once you turn your iPod into an external hard drive, you have to treat it like one by formally ejecting the drive from iTunes before disconnecting the iPod. (Do so by clicking the Eject icon next to the iPod's name in the iTunes Source list to safely free it and avoid huffy alert boxes from your operating system about improper device removal.)

Your music, movies, and other iTunes stuff are kept in a special, invisible place on the iPod, so copying regular computer files onto the iPod doesn't affect them. (And syncing your music with the Mac or PC doesn't affect the computer files, either.) However, remember that the more you fill up your iPod with entertainment, the less room you have to store data files—and vice versa.

Note A Mac can read a Windows-formatted iPod or iPod Nano, but Windows can't read the Mac disk format. If you want to use your iPod with both systems, plug it into the PC first and let it format itself for Windows. The Shuffle and the Touch automatically work with both Macs and PCs.

Read Text Files on the iPod

The squint factor may be a little much, but the iPod Classic or Nano can also lend its screen for displaying text files, which comes in handy if you want to review class notes while relaxing or skim your talking points before a presentation.

You create iPod Notes from plain text files (with a *.txt* extension) like those from Windows NotePad or TextEdit on a Mac. You can't use full-fledged word-processing documents from Microsoft Word or AppleWorks, unless you save them as plain text files.

To use the iPod's Notes feature:

❶ Connect the iPod to the computer as an external disk. (Flip back two pages to find out how.)

❷ Once you've saved your text files in the proper plain-text format, open the iPod by double-clicking its icon on the Mac desktop or in the My Computer window.

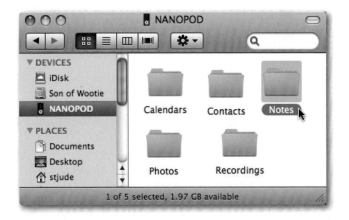

> **Note** By itself, the iPod can only display short text files under 4 kilobytes in size, but there's plenty of shareware around the Web that lets you read much longer files on your iPod. Hit the links at *www.missingmanuals.com* to see a few options.

❸ Drag the files into the Notes folder on the iPod.

❹ After you've copied your text files, eject the iPod from iTunes by clicking the Eject button next to its name in the Source list (or use the Eject button in the corner of the iTunes window).

❺ When you're ready to start reading, choose Extras→Notes. You'll see the names of your text files listed in the Notes menu. Scroll to the one you want and click the iPod's center button to bring it onscreen.

As you read, you can use the scroll wheel to page up and down through the file. Press the Menu button to close the file and return to the list of Notes files. If you can't find a document you're looking for in the Notes menu, open the Notes folder on the iPod and make sure it is indeed a *.txt* file.

Boswell's Life of Johnson highlights.txt

Mr. Cambridge, upon this, politely said, 'Dr. Johnson, I am going, with your pardon, to accuse myself, for I have the same custom which I perceive you have. But it seems odd that one should have such a desire to look at the backs of books.' Johnson, ever ready for contest, instantly started from his reverie, wheeled about, and answered, 'Sir, the reason is very plain. Knowledge is of two kinds. We know a subject ourselves, or we know where we can find information upon it. When we enquire into any subject, the first thing we have to do is to know what books have treated of it. This leads us to look at catalogues, and the backs of books in libraries.'

Using the iPod as a text reader is a handy way to bring along your grocery list so you can rock while you shop. If you want to browse more challenging prose than "Buy Pampers," though, swing by Project Gutenberg's Web site at *www.gutenberg.us*. Here, you can download thousands of public-domain literary works as plain text files and transfer them into your iPod's Notes folder for a little Shakespeare, Schopenhauer, or Sun Tzu.

Tip The iPod Touch may not be able to double as an external hard disk (and thus, a pocket ebook reader) without help from third-party software, but if you've got a Wi-Fi signal, who needs a hard disk? Since you, Touch owner, have the Web in the palm of your hand, just point your mini-Safari directly at *gutenberg.us* or *books.google.com* to do your reading. If you've got an online text storage locker like Google Docs (*docs.google.com*), you can stash personal files and notes in there and then tap them open to read when you log into your Google account. And don't forget the 99-cent classics in the Books section of the iTune App Store. Or the free Shakespeare app, where you can get the complete works of The Bard in less than 3 megabytes of precious Touch space.

Surfing the Web with iPod Touch

I f you have an iPod Touch, you have something that no other iPod has: the power of the World Wide Web, right in your pocket. The Web on the iPod Touch looks like the Web on your computer, and that's one of Apple's greatest accomplishments. You see the real deal—the actual fonts, graphics, and layouts—not the stripped-down, bare-bones mini-Web you usually get on cellphone screens.

The iPod Touch's Web browser is Safari, a lite version of the same one that comes with every Macintosh and is now available for Windows. It's fast, simple to use, and very pretty indeed. This chapter will show you how to get online with your Touch, and then what to do once you get there.

Get Your Wi-Fi Connection

Before you can get surfin' with Safari, you need to get the iPod Touch connected to the Internet. This means you have to connect it to a *Wi-Fi* network. Wi-Fi, known to the geeks as 802.11 and to Apple fans as AirPort, means wireless networking. It's the same technology that lets laptops the world over get online at high speed in any Wi-Fi *hot spot*. Hot spots are everywhere these days: in homes, offices, coffee shops (notably Starbucks), hotels, airports, and thousands of other places.

When you're in a Wi-Fi hot spot, your iPod Touch has a very fast connection to the Internet, as though it's connected to a cable modem or DSL. In fact, if you connect your iPod Touch to your own home wireless network, it's actually using that same cable or DSL connection that your other computers around the house are sharing amongst themselves.

When you launch any of the Touch's programs that require an Internet connection—Safari or YouTube, for example—the iPod tries to get online following this sequence:

- First, it sniffs around for a Wi-Fi network that you've used before. If it finds one, it connects quietly and automatically. You're not asked for permission, a password, or anything else.

- If the iPod can't find a previous hot spot, but it detects a *new* hot spot, a message appears on the screen. It displays the new hot spot's name; tap it to connect. (If you see a 🔒 icon next to the hot spot's name, then it's been protected by a password, which you'll have to enter on the keyboard that pops up.)

Silencing the "Select a Wi-Fi Network" Messages

Every now and then, you might be bombarded by those "Select a Wi-Fi Network" messages, at a time when you have no need to be online. You might want the iPod to stop bugging you—to *stop* offering Wi-Fi hot spots.

In that situation, from the Home screen, tap Settings→Wi-Fi and turn off "Ask to Join Networks". When this option is off, the iPod never blares out the names of new networks for you to join. You always have to visit this Settings screen and select a network each time you want join a new network, as described next.

The List of Hot Spots

At some street corners in big cities, Wi-Fi signals bleeding out of apartment buildings sometimes give you a choice of 20 or 30 hot spots to join. But whenever the iPod invites you to join a hot spot, it suggests only a couple of them: the ones with the strongest signal and, if possible, no password requirement.

But you might sometimes want to see the complete list of available hot spots—maybe because the iPod-suggested hot spot is flaky. To see the full list, from the Home screen, tap Settings→Wi-Fi. Tap the one you want to join.

Commercial Hot Spots

Tapping the name of the hot spot you want to join is generally all you have to do—if it's a home Wi-Fi network. Unfortunately, joining a *commercial* Wi-Fi hot spot—one that requires a credit-card number (in a hotel room or airport, for example)—requires more than just connecting to it. You also have to *sign into* it, exactly as you'd do if you were using a laptop.

To do that, return to the Home screen and open Safari. You'll see the "Enter your payment information" screen either immediately, or as soon as you try to open a Web page of your choice.

Supply your credit-card information or (if you have a membership to this Wi-Fi chain, like Boingo or T-Mobile) your name and password. Click Submit or Proceed, try *not* to contemplate how this $8 per hour is pure profit for somebody, and enjoy your surfing.

Going on a Safari Tour

You get onto the Web by tapping the Safari icon on the Home screen (below, left); the very first time you do this, a blank browser window appears (below, right). To type a Web address into the browser, tap the address bar and the keyboard pops up on screen ready for your input.

Safari has most of the features of a desktop Web browser: bookmarks, auto-complete (for Web addresses), cookies, a pop-up ad blocker, and so on. (It's missing niceties like password memorization and multimedia plug-ins.)

When you go to a Web page, mini-Safari behaves just like a desktop browser. It highlights the address bar as it loads all the elements on the page, and even gives you Apple's circular "Wait! Wait! I'm loading the page!" animated icon at the top of the screen.

> **Note** Depending on when you got your Touch and how often you update its software, you may see certain icons in different places on the screen—especially in the Safari browser, which Apple likes to tinker with. You may, for example, see a separate search bar next to the address bar and a relocated Refresh button.

Here's a quick tour of the main screen elements, starting from the upper left:

- **Q (Search).** Tap here to have a Search box unfold below the Safari address bar. Type in your keywords and tap the blue Google (or Yahoo) button that appears in the bottom-right corner.

- **Address bar.** This empty white box is where you enter the *URL* (Web address) for a page you want to visit. (URL is short for the even less self-explanatory Uniform Resource Locator.)

- **✗, ↻ (Stop, Reload).** Click the ✗ button to interrupt the downloading of a Web page you've just requested (if you've made a mistake, for instance, or if it's taking too long).

Once a page has finished loading, the ✗ button turns into a ↻ button. Click this circular arrow if a page doesn't look or work quite right, or if you want to see the updated version of a Web page (such as a breaking-news site) that changes constantly. Safari re-downloads the Web page and reinterprets its text and graphics.

- **◀, ▶ (Back, Forward).** Tap the ◀ button to revisit the page you were just on.

  Once you've tapped ◀, you can then tap the ▶ button to return to the page you were on *before* you tapped the ◀ button.

- **✚ (Add Bookmark).** When you're on a page that you might want to visit again later, bookmark it by tapping this button.

- **(Bookmarks).** This button brings up your list of saved bookmarks (skip ahead a few pages to read more about bookmarks).

- **(Page Juggler).** Safari can keep multiple Web pages open, just like any other browser. The number indicates how many open pages you've got.

Zoom and Scroll Through Web Pages

These two gestures—zooming in on Web pages and then scrolling around them—have probably sold more people on the iPhone and the iPod Touch than any other feature. It all happens with a fluid animation, and a responsiveness to your finger taps, that's positively addicting. New owners often spend time just zooming in and out of Web pages, simply because they can.

When you first open a Web page, you get to see the *entire thing*. Unlike Web browsers on most cellphones, the Touch crams the entire Web site onto its 3.5-inch screen, so you can get the lay of the land.

At this point, of course, you're looking at .004-point type, which is too small to read unless you're a microbe. So the next step is to magnify the *part* of the page you want to read.

The iPod Touch offers three ways to do that:

- **Rotate the iPod.** Turn the device 90 degrees in either direction. The Touch rotates and magnifies the image to fill the wider view.

- **Do the two-finger spread.** Put two fingers on the glass and drag them apart. The Web page stretches before your very eyes, growing larger. Then you can pinch to shrink the page back down again. (Most people do several spreads or several pinches in a row to achieve the degree of zoom they want.)

- **Double-tap.** Safari is intelligent enough to recognize different *chunks* of a Web page. One article might represent a chunk. A photograph might qualify as a chunk. When you double-tap a chunk, Safari magnifies *just that chunk* to fill the whole screen. It's smart and useful.

Double-tap again to zoom back out.

Double-tap

Once you've zoomed out to the proper degree, you can then scroll around the page by dragging or flicking with a finger. You don't have to worry about "clicking a link" by accident; if your finger's in motion, Safari ignores the tapping action, even if you happen to land on a link. It's awesome.

To go ahead and actually click a link, simply tap it with your finger.

Tip Every now and then, you'll find, on a certain Web page, a *frame* (a column of text) with its own scroll bar—an area that scrolls independently of the main page. (If you have a MobileMe account, for example, the Messages list is such a frame.)

The Touch has a secret, undocumented method for scrolling one of these frames without scrolling the whole page: the *two-finger drag*. Check it out.

The Safari Address Bar

As on a computer, this Web browser offers four ways to navigate the Web:

• Type an address into the Address bar.

• Choose a bookmark.

• Return to a site you've visited recently, using the History list.

• Tap a link.

The following pages cover each of these methods in turn.

The Address bar is the strip at the top of the screen where you type in a Web page's address. And it so happens that *three* of the iPod Touch's greatest tips and shortcuts all have to do with this important navigational tool:

• **Insta-scroll to the top.** You can jump directly to the Address bar, no matter how far down a page you've scrolled, just by tapping the very top edge of the screen (on the status bar). That "tap the top" trick is timely, too, when a Web site *hides* the Address bar.

Tap anywhere on this strip...   *...to jump back to the top of the page.*

- **Don't delete.** There *is* an  button at the right end of the Address bar, whose purpose is to erase the entire current address so you can type another one. (Tap inside the Address bar to make it, and the keyboard, appear.) But the ⊗ button is for suckers.

  Instead, whenever the Address is open for typing, *just type*. Forget that there's already a URL there—just start typing. The iPod is smart enough to figure out that you want to *replace* that Web address with a new one.

- **Don't type** *http://www or .com.*
  Safari is smart enough to know that most Web addresses begin and end with those terms—so you can leave all that stuff out, and it will supply them automatically. Instead of *http://www.cnn.com*, for example, just type *cnn* and hit Go. (If the suffix you seek is .net, .edu, or .org, press and hold the .com button and slide across to the one you need, as shown at right.)

Otherwise, this Address bar works just like the one in any other Web browser. Tap inside it to make the keyboard appear. (If the Address bar is hidden, tap the top edge of the Touch's screen.)

Flip the page for more about using the Touch keyboard.

Use the Touch Keyboard

The iPod Touch has no physical keys—heck, it barely has any actual buttons. A virtual keyboard, therefore, is the only possible system for entering text.

The keyboard appears automatically whenever you tap in a place where typing is possible, mainly in the address bar of the Web browser or within a Web page itself. You can also use it when emailing (Chapter 3) and to enter calendar appointments and contact information (Chapter 10).

To use it, just tap the key you want. As your finger taps the glass, a "speech balloon" appears above your finger, showing an enlarged version of the key you actually hit (since your finger is now blocking your view of the keyboard).

In darker gray, surrounding the letters, you'll find these special keys:

❶ **Shift (⇧).** When you tap this key, it glows white, to indicate that it's in effect. The next letter you type appears as a capital. Then the ⇧ key automatically returns to normal, meaning that the next letter will be lowercase.

❷ **Backspace (⌫).** This key actually has three speeds.

- Tap it once to delete the letter just before the blinking insertion point.

- Hold it down to "walk" backward, deleting as you go.

- If you hold down the key long enough, it starts deleting *words* rather than letters, one whole chunk at a time.

❸ **?123** . Tap this button when you want to type numbers or punctuation. The keyboard changes to offer a palette of numbers and symbols. Tap the same key—which now says ABC—to return to the letters keyboard. (Fortunately, there's a much faster way to get a period—just touch the **?123** key and slide your finger up to the number you need, then let go.)

Once you're on the numbers/symbols pad, a new dark gray button appears, labeled **#+=**. Tapping it summons a *third* keyboard layout, containing the less frequently used characters, like brackets, the # and % symbols, bullets, and math symbols.

When you're typing in a Web form (or someplace that's not a Web address), the keyboard also adds a Return key. Tapping this key moves to the next line, just as on a real keyboard.

Surfing on the Safari Keyboard

Safari is the only spot on the Touch where you can *rotate* the keyboard into landscape orientation. This is a big deal; when it's stretched out the wide way, you get much bigger, broader keys, and typing is much easier and faster. Just remember to rotate the iPod *before* you tap into the Address bar or text box; once the keyboard is on the screen, you can't rotate the image.

As you probably know, there are no spaces allowed in Internet addresses; therefore, in the spot usually reserved for the Space bar, this keyboard has three keys for things that *do* appear often in Web addresses: period, /, and ".com". These nifty special keys make typing Web addresses a lot faster.

Finally, tap the blue Go key when you're finished typing the address. That's your Enter key. (Or tap Cancel to hide the keyboard *without* "pressing Enter.")

As you type, a handy list of suggestions appears beneath the Address bar. These are all Web addresses that Safari already knows about, either because they're in your Bookmarks list or in your History list (meaning you've visited them recently).

If you recognize the address you're trying to type, by all means tap it instead of typing out the rest of the URL. The time you save could be your own.

Create and Use Safari Bookmarks

Amazingly enough, Safari comes pre-stocked with bookmarks (Favorites)—that is, a list of Web sites you might want to visit again without having to remember and type their URLs. Even more amazingly, all of these canned bookmarks are interesting and useful to *you* in particular! How did it know?

Easy—it copied your existing desktop computer's browser bookmarks from Internet Explorer (Windows) or Safari (Macintosh and Windows) when you synced the Touch. Sneaky, eh? (Flip ahead a few pages if you haven't synced.)

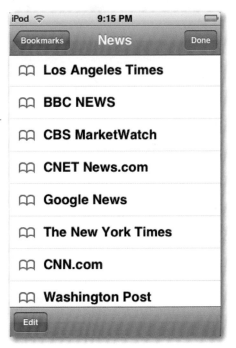

Anyway, to see the bookmarks, tap the button at the bottom of the screen. You see the master list of bookmarks. Some may be "loose," and many more are probably organized into folders, or even folders *within* folders. Tapping a folder shows you what's inside, and tapping a bookmark immediately begins opening the corresponding Web site.

> **Tip** The iPod Touch has a Caps Lock feature, but you have to request it. Press the Home button and go to Settings→General→Keyboard and turn on "Enable caps lock." From now on, if you double-tap the ⇧ key, it turns blue. You're now in Caps Lock mode, and you'll now type in ALL CAPITALS until you tap the ⇧ key again. (If you can't seem to make Caps Lock work, try double-tapping the ⇧ key *fast.*)
>
> You can also turn on (or off) the Auto-Capitalization feature here, plus the shortcut that inserts a period followed by a space when you tap the space bar twice.

Adding New Bookmarks

You can add new bookmarks right on the phone. Any work you do here is copied *back* to your computer the next time you sync the two machines.

When you find a Web page you might like to visit again, tap the **+** button (bottom center of the screen). Tap the Add Bookmark option. The Add Bookmark screen appears. You have two tasks:

- **Type a better name.** In the top box, you can type a shorter or clearer name for the page than the one it comes with. Instead of "Bass, Trout, & Tackle—the Web's Premiere Resource for the Avid Outdoorsman," you can just call it "Fish site."

  The box below this one identifies the underlying URL, which is totally independent from what you've *called* your bookmark. You can't edit this one.

- **Specify where to file this bookmark.** If you tap the button that says Bookmarks >, you open Safari's hierarchical list of bookmark folders, which organize your bookmarked sites. Tap the folder where you want to file the new bookmark, so you'll know where to find it later.

> **Tip** If you make a typo when tapping in a URL and don't notice it right away, you don't have to backspace all the way back to it. Press your finger down on the text until a magnifying glass and a flashing insertion cursor appear, then drag your finger back to the error, plant the cursor, and correct it. Then go back to where you were.

Edit and Organize Bookmarks and Folders

It's easy enough to massage your Bookmarks list—to delete favorites that aren't so favorite any more, make new folders, rearrange the list, rename a folder or a bookmark, and so on.

The techniques are the same for editing bookmark *folders* and editing the bookmarks themselves—after the first step. To edit the folder list, start by opening the Bookmarks list (tap the ⌘ button), and then tap Edit.

To edit the bookmarks themselves, tap the ⌘ button, tap a folder, and *then* tap Edit.

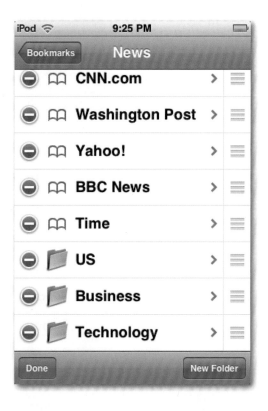

> **Tip** Want to add your favorite Web site to your Home screen? Tap the + button at the bottom of your browser and choose "Add to Home Screen". The site's icon is now right on the Touch's main screen. And don't worry about filling up your Home screen—you can have up to nine of 'em and finger-flick between them.

Now you can:

- **Delete something.** Tap the ⊖ button next to a folder or bookmark, and then tap Delete to confirm.

- **Rearrange the list.** Drag the grip strip (≡) up or down in the list to move the folders or bookmarks up or down. (You can't move or delete the top three folders—History, Bookmarks Bar, and Bookmarks Menu.)

iPod 📶	9:25 PM	🔋

‹ Bookmarks	**News**	
⊖ 📖 **CNN.com**	›	≡
⊖ 📖 **The New York Ti...**	›	≡
⊖ 📖 **Los Angeles Ti...**	›	≡
⊖ 📖 **BBC NEWS**	›	≡
⊖ 📖 **CBS MarketWatch**	›	≡
⊖ 📖 **CNET News.com**	›	≡
⊖ 📖 **Google News**	›	≡
⊖ 📖 **The New York Ti...**	›	≡
Done		New Folder

- **Edit a name and location.** Tap a folder or bookmark name. If you tapped a folder, you arrive at the Edit Folder screen, which lets you edit the folder's name and which folder it's *inside* of. If you tapped a bookmark, you see the Edit Bookmark screen, where you can edit the name and the URL it points to.

  Tap the Back button (upper-left corner) when you're finished.

- **Create a folder.** Tap the New Folder button in the lower-right corner of the Edit Folders screen. You're offered the chance to type a name for it and to specify where you want to file it (that is, in which *other* folder).

Tap Done when you're finished.

Syncing Bookmarks with iTunes

Bookmarks—those helpful little point-and-click shortcuts that have saved us all countless hours of mistyping Web site addresses—are a reflection of your personality, because they generally tend to be sites that are important to *you*. Fortunately, they can make the trip to your iPod Touch, too. In fact, any bookmarks you create on the iPod can eventually be copied back to your computer, too; it's a two-way street.

iTunes can transfer your bookmarks from Internet Explorer or Safari. Just plug in the iPod Touch, click its icon in iTunes, and click the Info tab. Scroll down past Contacts, Calendars, and Mail Accounts until you get to the section called Web Browser. Then:

- **In Windows,** turn on *Sync bookmarks from:*, and then choose either *Safari* or *Internet Explorer* from the pop-up menu. Click Apply to sync.

- **On the Mac,** turn on *Sync Safari bookmarks* and click Apply.

If you ever want to blow away all the bookmarks on your Touch and start over with a fresh set of bookmarks from your computer, scroll down to the Advanced area of the Info screen (where it says "Replace information on this iPod"). Then put a check in the box next to Bookmarks before you sync again.

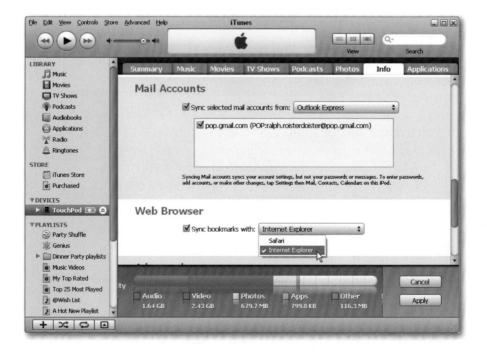

Special Instructions for Firefox Fans

If Mozilla's Firefox browser is your preferred window to the Web, you can still get those foxy favorites moved over to the iPod. But you'll have to do it the long way—by importing bookmarks from Firefox into Safari. And while this setup will get your bookmarks onto the iPod, it won't establish a *two-way* sync; new bookmarks you add on the iPod won't get synced back to Firefox.

- **Windows.** Download a free copy of Safari *www.apple.com/safari*, start it up, and let it import your Firefox bookmarks during the setup process. Once it does, press Ctrl+Alt+B to show all your bookmarks, weed out the ones you don't want, and then set the iPod Touch to sync with Safari.

- **Macintosh.** You already have Safari. If you have your whole bookmarked life in Firefox, grit your teeth and open that dusty Safari anyway, then choose File→Import Bookmarks. Navigate to your Firefox book- marks file, which is usually in your Home folder→Library→Application Support→Firefox→Profiles→*weird scrambled-named folder like e9v01wmx. default* folder. Inside, double-click the file called bookmarks.html.

  You've just imported your Firefox bookmarks. Now, in Safari, press ⌘-Option-B to show all your bookmarks on screen. Delete the ones you don't want on the Touch, and then set the iPod to sync with Safari.

Actually, *most* other browsers can export their bookmarks. You can use that option to export your bookmarks file to your desktop, and then use Safari's File→Import Bookmarks menu to pull it from there.

The Safari History List

Behind the scenes, Safari keeps track of the Web sites you've visited in the last week or so, neatly organized into subfolders like Earlier Today and Yesterday. It's a great feature when you can't recall the URL for a Web site that you visited recently—or when you remember that it had a long, complicated address and you get the psychiatric condition known as iPod Touch Keyboard Dread.

To see the list of recent sites, tap the 🕮 button, and then tap the History folder, whose icon bears a little clock to make sure you know that it's special. Once the History list appears, just tap a bookmark (or a folder name and *then* a bookmark) to revisit that Web page.

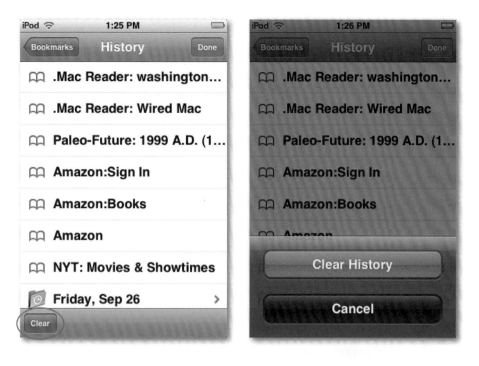

Erasing the History List

Some people find it creepy that Safari maintains a complete list of every Web site they've seen recently, right there in plain view of any family member or co-worker who wanders by. They'd just as soon their wife/husband/boss/parent/kid not know what Web sites they've been visiting.

You can't delete just one particularly incriminating History listing. You can, however, delete the *entire* History menu, thus erasing all of your tracks. To do that, tap Clear; confirm by tapping Clear History.

You've just rewritten History.

Tapping Links

You'd be surprised at the number of iPod Touch newbies who stare dumbly at the screen, awestruck at the beauty of full-blown Web pages—but utterly baffled as to how to click links.

The answer: Tap with your finger.

Just tap the links on the screen, much the way you'd click them if you had a mouse. As you know from desktop-computer browsing, not all links are blue and underlined. Sometimes, in fact, they're graphics.

Tip If you hold your finger on a link for a moment—touching rather than tapping—a handy bubble sprouts from it, identifying the full Web address that will open. For example, the link might *say,* "For a good time, click here," but it might actually take you to a Web site like *www.missingmanuals.com.*

Mapping Your Way with Wi-Fi

People who bought the first version of the iPod Touch had to use Safari for all their map work and driving directions. Owners of 2008 iPod Touches (and those who paid Apple $10 or $20 to upgrade their software on their 2007 models) can use the built-in Maps app instead. Like Safari, though, Maps needs a Wi-Fi connection to pull its data down from the Web, so it's not the best thing in the world for emergency directions when you're lost in the bad part of town.

To plot your course, tap the Maps icon on the Home screen. Here are some of the things you can do with Maps and a network connection:

- **Find yourself.** Tap the icon in the bottom-left corner (circled) to have the Touch pinpoint your current location within a few hundred yards. (While it doesn't have a GPS chip inside, it does have software that calculates your position based on a big database of Wi-Fi hotspots.)

- **Find an address.** In the Address box at the top of the screen, type in an address—or tap the 🕮 icon to call up your Contacts list, where you can select the friend or business you want to map. Tap the Search button to see a red pushpin drop on that location.

- **Find your way.** Tap the Directions button at the bottom of the screen. A two-field box appears. If you don't want to use your current location, tap the ⊗ in the Start box and type in a point of origin. In the End box, type in the destination address. Press the Route button. This gives you a map to follow, but if you'd like text-based instructions, tap the icon on the bottom right corner (circled) to peel back the screen. Here, tap List to get a written explanation of your route. You can also choose the look of your map: a regular cartographic version, a satellite image, or a hybrid of both. Tap Show Traffic if you want to see current road congestion and maybe take that antacid *before* you leave the house.

Search the Web

You don't have to look far to find a search engine on the Touch's version of Safari. Just tap the magnifying-glass icon (that looks like Q) to pop open a Search box right below the main Address Bar.

That's an awfully handy shortcut. It means that you can perform a Google search without having to go to Google.com first. Just tap into that box, type your search phrase, and then tap the big blue Google box in the lower-right corner.

> **Tip** At first glance, the Touch keyboard may look like it can't handle accented letters like é or ü, but looks can be deceiving. The trick to getting those graves, acutes, umlauts, tildes, and other diacritical marks on your typed characters? As shown above, hold down the key for an extra second or two and a whole world of accents appears on screen. Just slide your fingertip over to the one you want. Voilà!

Changing the Default Search Engine

But say, for some reason, you don't like Google. You're a Yahoo fan and would rather do your exploring with your preferred search engine.

Are you stuck with Google on your iPod Touch? Nope, not at all.

You can tell the iPod to use Yahoo's search feature instead of Google, if you like. From the Home screen, tap Settings→Safari→Search Engine. Once you get in there, tap Yahoo. If you ever want to change it back to Google, just return to the Settings menu.

Tip There are all kinds of cool things you can type in the Google search bar to get immediate feedback from Google—special terms that tell Google, "I want *information*, not Web-page matches."

For example, you can type a movie name and zip code or city/state (*The Titanic Returns 10024*) to get an immediate list of today's showtimes in theaters near you. Get the forecast by typing *weather chicago* or *weather 60609*. Stock quotes: just type the stock symbol (*amzn*). Dictionary definitions: *define schadenfreude*. Unit conversions: *liters in 5 gallons*. Currency conversions: *25 usd in euros*.

Then tap the blue Google button to get instant results. And, yes, many of the same shortcuts work on Yahoo as well.

Audio and Video on the Web

In general, streaming audio and video on the Touch is a bust. The Touch doesn't recognize the Real or Windows Media file formats, nor does it understand Flash. All of this means that the iPod can't easily play the huge majority of online video and audio recordings.

But the iPod Touch isn't *utterly* clueless about streaming online goodies. It can play some QuickTime movies, like movie trailers, as long as they've been encoded (prepared) in certain formats (like H.264). It can also play MP3 and WAV audio files right off the Web. Here are a few sites to sample:

- **BBC News.** The Beeb's podcasts stream nicely when you tap the Podcast icon and then the Download link. *http://www.bbc.co.uk/radio/ podcasts/directory/station/worldservice/*

- **New York Times podcasts.** A whole page of different news shows that start streaming when you tap the MP3 link. *www.nytimes.com/podcasts*

- **"Meet the Press" audio stream.** An MP3 edition of the venerable Sunday morning talk show can be found here: *http://podcast.msnbc.com/audio/ podcast/MSNBC-MTP.xml*

Actually, any old MP3 file plays fine right in Safari. If you've already played through your 8, 16, or 32 gigabytes of music synced from your computer, you can always do a Web search for *free mp3 music*.

As for video, you have more to watch on the Web than just Touch-friendly streaming videos that you can get back at Home→YouTube. Apple, in addition to making iPods and Macs, also hosts a huge collection of movie trailers on its site at *www.apple.com/trailers*. Tap a movie poster to get started.

Tip If you're dreaming of streaming Internet radio over the Touch's Wi-Fi waves, check out the App Store. There, you can find free Touchable versions of Pandora Internet Radio, the Minnesota Public Radio player, and AOL Radio (200 music stations and 150 CBS Radio stations with plenty of news, talk, and sports).

Social Networking on the iPod Touch

With your iPod Touch, you can keep connected to all your favorite social networking sites anywhere you can hop onto a wireless network. But if you find the Web versions of Facebook, MySpace, or Twitter a little unwieldy on the Touch screen, you have another option: App Store editions of your online hangouts.

Chapter 7 has info about the Store and Chapter 3 has instructions on how to install iPod Touch apps. Once you're ready, here's some of what's out there:

- **Facebook** and **MySpace.** Both mega-popular destinations have free mobile applications, right there in the App Store. Customized with easy to read text and big tappable icons, these mobile versions were designed to look good on the iPhone and iPod Touch. Once you download and install the app, you just need to fire it up and log in like you do on the regular site.

Facebook

- **Twitter.** Using this widely popular micro-blogging service is much more fun on the iPod Touch than trying to text out pithy thoughts on a tiny mobile phone keypad (unless, of course, it's an iPhone). Several free Twitter-friendly programs are available in the App Store, including *Twitterific*, *Twittelator*, and *TwitterFon*. For a global perspective, the *Twittervision* program lets you see tweets from around the world.

Exposure

- **Flickr.** Browsing the pictures on this massive photo-sharing site is nice and easy with *Exposure*, which neatly arranges images and info vertically on the Touch screen, with fullscreen views on tap. Icons to your photos, your contacts' photos, and Flickr's featured photos line the bottom of the screen, along with a Near Me button that uses your current location to round up pictures taken nearby.

- **LOLCats.** Those wacky felines have at least two applications to show off their ungrammatical exploits as submitted by hundreds of cat owners. If you need to take a break and have a laugh at kitty's expense, try *LOLCats* or *LOLCats Free*.

LOLCats Free

Manipulate Multiple Pages

Like any self-respecting browser, Safari can keep multiple pages open at once, making it easy for you to switch between them. You can think of it as a miniature version of *tabbed browsing*, the feature you find on Safari Senior, Firefox, and the latest Internet Explorer, which keeps a bunch of Web pages open simultaneously—in a single, neat window.

The beauty of this arrangement is that you can start reading one Web page while the others load into their own tabs in the background. On the iPod Touch, it works like this:

- **To open a new window,** tap the ⬚ button in the lower right. The Web page shrinks into a mini version. Tap New Page to open a new, untitled Web-browser page; now you can enter an address or whatever.

> **Note** Touch Safari can handle eight open Web pages at once. If you try to go for that ninth one, you'll get a message that you have too many pages open. The solution? Tap your Page Juggler and close some pages.

- **To switch back to the first window,** tap  again. Now there are two dots (• •) beneath the miniature page, indicating that *two* windows are open. (The boldest, whitest dot indicates where you are in the horizontal row of windows.) Bring the first window's miniature onto the screen by flicking horizontally with your finger. Tap it to open it full-screen.

  You can open a third window, and a fourth, and so on, and jump between them, using these two techniques. The ⬜ icon sprouts a number to let you know how many windows are open; for example, it might say ⬛.

- **To close a window,** tap ⬜. Flick over to the tiny window you want to close, and then tap the ✖ button at its top-left corner.

Note Sometimes, Safari sprouts a new window *automatically* when you click a link. That's because the link you tapped is programmed to open a new window.

Pop-up Blockers, Cookies, and Security

The world's smarmiest advertisers have been inundating us with pop-up and pop-under ads for years—nasty little windows that appear in front of the browser window, or, worse, behind it, waiting to jump out the moment you close your window. They're often deceptive, masquerading as error messages or dialog boxes, and they'll do absolutely anything to get you to click them.

Fortunately for you, Safari comes set to block those pop-ups so you don't see them. It's a war out there—but at least you have some ammunition.

The thing is, though, pop-ups are sometimes legitimate (and not ads)—notices of new banking features, seating charts on ticket-sales sites, warnings that the instructions for using a site have changed, and so on. Safari can't tell these from ads—and it stifles them too. So if a site you trust says "Please turn off pop-up blockers and reload this page," you know you're probably missing out on a *useful* pop-up message.

In those situations, you can turn off the pop-up blocker. From the Home screen, tap Settings→Safari. Where it says "Block Pop-ups," tap the On/Off switch.

Cookies

Cookies are something like Web page preference files. Certain Web sites—particularly commercial ones like Amazon.com—deposit them on your hard drive like little bookmarks, so they'll remember you the next time you visit. Ever notice how Amazon.com greets you "Welcome, Leroy" (or whatever your name is)? It's reading its own cookie, left behind on your hard drive (or in this case, on your iPod).

Most cookies are perfectly innocuous—and, in fact, are extremely helpful, because they help Web sites remember your tastes. Cookies also spare you the effort of having to type in your name, address, and so on, every time you visit these Web sites.

But fear is widespread, and the media fans the flames with tales of sinister cookies that track your movement on the Web. If you're worried about invasions of privacy, Safari is ready to protect you.

To check all this out, from the Home screen, tap Settings→Safari. The options here are like a paranoia gauge. If you click Never, you create an acrylic shield around your iPod. No cookies can come in, and no cookie information can go out. You'll probably find the Web a very inconvenient place; you'll have to re-enter your information upon every visit, and some Web sites may not work properly at all. The Always option means, "oh, what the heck—just gimme all of them."

A good compromise is From Visited, which accepts cookies from sites you *want* to visit, but blocks cookies deposited on your Touch by sites you're not actually visiting—cookies you get, say, from an especially evil banner ad that's been planted on a page by hackers, for example. There are quite a few of those these days.

The Safari settings screen also offers a Clear Cookies button (deletes all the cookies you've accumulated so far), as well as Clear History and Clear Cache.

The *cache* is a little patch of the Touch's storage area where bits and pieces of Web pages you visit—graphics, for example—are retained. The idea is that the next time you visit the same page, the iPod won't have to download those bits again. It's already got them on board, so the page appears much faster.

If you worry that your cache eats up space, poses a security risk, or is confusing some page (by preventing the most recent version of the page from appearing), tap this button to erase it and start over.

RSS: The Missing Manual

In the beginning, the Internet was an informational Garden of Eden. There were no banner ads, pop-ups, flashy animations, or spam messages. Back then, people thought the Internet was the greatest idea ever.

Those days, alas, are long gone. Web browsing now entails a constant battle against intrusive advertising and annoying animations. And with the proliferation of Web sites of every kind—from news sites to personal blogs—just reading your favorite sites can become a full-time job.

Enter RSS, a technology that lets you subscribe to *feeds*—summary blurbs provided by thousands of sources around the world, from Reuters to Apple to your nerdy next-door neighbor. The result: You spare yourself the tediousness of checking for updates manually, plus you get to read short summaries of new articles without ads and blinking animations. And if you want to read a full article, you just tap its headline.

Safari, as it turns out, doubles as a handy RSS reader. Whenever you tap an "RSS Feed" link on a Web page, or whenever you type the address of an RSS feed into the Address bar (it often begins with *feed://*), Safari automatically displays a handy table-of-contents view that lists all of the news blurbs on that page.

Scan the summaries—and when you see an article that looks intriguing, tap its headline. You go to the full-blown Web page to read the full-blown article.

Tip It's worth bookmarking your favorite RSS feeds. One great one for tech fans is *feed://www.digg.com/rss/index.xml*, a constantly updated list of the coolest and most interesting tech and pop-culture stories of the day. Most news publications offer news feeds, too. (The humble author of this chapter has his own daily *New York Times* feed at *http://pogue.blogs.nytimes.com/?feed=rss2*.)

Find Other Mobile-Friendly Sites

If looking at regular Web pages on your iPod's browser is too much sensory overload, and RSS is a little too sparse, you have some middle ground. There are many Web sites out there that have been *optimized* for use on mobile devices, like cellphones, wireless PDAs, iPhones, and Touch iPods.

These sites offer large type (all the better to read on pee-wee screens) and a quick-loading graphic or two. But how do you find these little treasures?

Some big Web sites can automatically sense when you're coming in on a mobile browser and will serve you up the simplified version. Others will swap out the *www* part of the URL with an *m* (for mobile), as in *m.nytimes.com*.

Here are a few sites with mobile browsers in mind:

- Google (of course) has mobile versions of many of its features, like Gmail and Picasa online photo albums, at *www.google.com/mobile*.

- The British Broadcasting Corporation has a streamlined version of its main news site at *www.bbc.co.uk/mobile*.

- Yahoo has its mobile offerings, including streamlined search, sports, and stock quotes, at *m.yahoo.com*.

- There are also Web pages that round up links to the mobile editions of popular sites. Here are two worth bookmarking on your Touch browser: *www.cantoni.mobi/* and *mobile.palm.com*.

iPod Out Loud

Now that you've spent all that time getting your iPod fully loaded, you probably want to listen to your playlists, albums, audio books, and podcasts wherever you happen to be—in the car, on your big booming home stereo, in the bathroom, wherever. If you can load it onto your iPod, you can channel it through most any sound system—and it's not even that expensive, either. This chapter explains the simple procedures for playing your iPod songs through the woofers and tweeters in your life. (If you want to play iPod movies on your TV, flip back to Chapter 8).

One note of caution before plunking down your hard-earned cash on that fancy audio gizmo: Apple has made a lot of different iPod models over the years, and not every add-on and accessory out there works with all iPods. To be safe (especially if you recently bought a new iPod), check the product's fine print to make sure it and your iPod will be happy together.

Checklist: Taking the iPod on the Road

Since the glorious days of crackly AM radio, music and driving have gone hand in hand. These days, a stereo system with an AM/FM radio and a cassette deck is the bare minimum for most cars, and late-model vehicles now cruise around with all sorts of high-end equipment, from MP3-compatible CD players to satellite radio. (Whether the music you can play on them has improved over the years is still subject to debate.)

If having your playlists with you is your idea of paradise by the dashboard light, you have several inexpensive ways to integrate your iPod with your car's stereo. Whatever method you choose, you have to consider two factors:

- **How to connect your iPod to your existing audio system.** You have your pick of using either a cable or a wireless connection.

- **How to power your iPod.** Of course, your iPod can run fine on its battery for short trips. If you're retracing historic Route 66, however, you'll probably want to invest in an adapter that can power your iPod from the car's electrical system.

You've got four main ways to get your iPod piping through the car speakers, some of them more expensive than others. Here are the typical options, with further explanations on the less self-explanatory methods over the next few pages:

- **Using an FM transmitter.** These inexpensive devices let you borrow an empty frequency from your car's radio and play the iPod's music over the airwaves—no cables snaking across the dashboard required.
Advantages: Convenience; everybody's got an FM radio.
Disadvantages: Long road trippers constantly have to search for new frequencies. Urban dwellers may find it tough finding available signals.
Audio quality: fair.

The XtremeMac InChargeFM provides steady power as it pumps the iPod's music through the FM radio. It works with any iPod that has the flat dock-connector port; $70 at www.xtrememac.com.

- **Using a wired adapter.** Another option—especially if your car still has a cassette player—is getting one of those cassette-shaped gadgets that plugs into the tape deck and offers a wire to plug into the iPod's headphones port. Griffin Technology, Belkin, and Sony all make 'em.
  Advantages: Simplicity; insert cassette and you're good to go.
  Disadvantages: Not everyone's got a cassette deck anymore.
  Audio quality: fair.

Still cruising with the cassette deck? The $15 Griffin Technology DirectDeck adapter brings your iPod and cassette deck together to make music though the iPod's dock connector. The DirectDeck is available at www.griffintechnology.com.

- **Using the auxiliary jack.** If your car's stereo console has a 3.5 mm jack as an auxiliary input, you can use a simple male-to-male miniplug audio cable to connect your iPod. Radio Shack, Griffin Technology, or Monster Cable can help you out here for less than $15.
  Advantages: High-quality sound.
  Disadvantages: You still have to control your iPod using its scrollwheel.
  Audio quality: great.

- **Using a special iPod aftermarket kit or custom installation.** If you really want fine sound and have the budget for it, several companies now offer special kits that add an iPod-friendly cable to your existing in-dash stereo system.
  Advantages: Great sound, easy to control.
  Disadvantages: None, aside from price.
  Audio quality: great.

The popularity of the iPod over the past few years has even led major automobile manufacturers to include iPod cables wired right into their new cars. So if you're in the market for new wheels anyway, why not ask about getting your *click wheel* on the road, too?

You can connect your iPod to several Pioneer car stereo systems with the Pioneer CD-IB100II iPod Interface Adapter. The dashboard display even shows the track titles and lets you shuffle songs. Check it out at www.pioneerelectronics.com.

The FM Connection: Play the iPod Through a Radio's Speakers

If you're not a fan of wires, you can buy a doohickey that lets you broadcast your iPod's tunes over any nearby radio (not just your car's). These so-called FM transmitters have their pros and cons. True, you don't have to deal with cables or cords snarling the dashboard and they're fairly inexpensive. But the sound quality can vary—it depends on the strength of the signal—and radio is frustratingly prone to interference (static). If you live in a radio-heavy metropolitan area like New York or Los Angeles, finding a usable empty frequency can be an exercise in frustration.

Still, if you think an FM transmitter is your ticket to ride, you have several choices, among them:

- **iTrip or iTrip Auto.** Griffin Technology makes several eye-catching gadgets designed to pump your music from your iPod Touch, Classic, or Nano through the dashboard. The $50 iTrip (right) plugs into the iPod's dock-connector port to transmit the FM signal and uses the iPod's battery for its juice. If you want a built-in charger with your FM frequencies, consider Griffin's iTrip Auto Universal ($60). All models are at *www.griffintechnology.com*.

- **Belkin TuneCast Auto.** Belkin has a whole slew of products to make your iPod loud and proud, including the $70 TuneCast Auto FM transmitter that connects through the dock connector port on the iPod. The 12-volt plug keeps the juice flowing and the built-in ClearScan technology scans the frequencies for the best open band to park your iPod on. You can find all of Belkin's iPod offerings at *www.belkin.com*.

Serious Car Audio Fans:
The Custom Installation

Automobile manufacturers and car audio specialists have also fallen under the iPod's sweet siren song and are even making modifications to accommodate it—if they don't sell models that already include iPod connectivity. Apple has a list of car makers that support iPod connections at *www.apple.com/ipod/carintegration.html* (pictured below), where there's also a link to after-market solutions to retrofit your car's sound system for iPodding.

Here are a few other solutions to satisfy your mobile iPod audio needs:

- **Alpine iPod Interface KCA-422i.** This contraption is a simple cable that charges the iPod battery and displays song information on your car stereo's screen. The Alpine iPod Interface KCA-422i costs around $30 and works with a handful of the company's source units—the industry name for the dashboard stereo—which start at about $200. The Alpine iPod Interface is compatible with dock-connecting iPods and can be installed by an Alpine-authorized car audio dealer. Check out *www.alpine-usa.com* for more information.

- **Pioneer CD-IB100II iPod Interface Adapter.** This $50 box-and-cable device marries iPods to Pioneer car stereo systems tagged with the "iPod Adapter Ready" label. Once connected, the dashboard display even shows the iPod's track titles and lets you shuffle songs. You can get all the details at *www.pioneerelectronics.com*.

Play the iPod Through Portable Speakers

You can hook up your iPod to a home audio system to share your sounds, but sometimes it's more convenient to get the iPod a set of speakers to call its own. Some speakers connect to the iPod's headphone jack with a stereo miniplug cable, while others connect to the iPod's dock connector port.

The price and quality of iPod speakers can range from $15 cheap plastic things at the grocery store to $300 systems from high-end audio companies like Bose, Altec Lansing, Sony, Tivoli, and others. Here are a few speakers to sample, but check the list at the end of the chapter for more places to find booming iPod accessories.

- **Altec Lansing Moondance Glow.** Listen to your Van Morrison tracks in mood lighting! The Glow, pictured above, can splash a variety of colors on the wall behind it and lets you combine your iPod with stereo speakers, an FM radio, and dual alarm clocks. It comes with its own remote and you can find it for $180 at *www.alteclansing.com*.

- **JBL On Stage 200ID.** Proving that speakers do not have to be square, JBL offers several circular sound systems in its On Stage line for iPod. Available in various colors, JBL's systems also charge the iPod's battery. Prices range from about $100 to $150; see them at *www.jbl.com*.

- **XtremeMac Tango Studio.** This affordable bookshelf speaker system also has an FM radio and comes with its own remote control. It fits the iPod Classic and Nano, as well as older dock-connecting Pods, and sells for $80 at *www.xtrememac.com*.

Play the iPod In Many Rooms at Once

Why settle for pumping the iPod's music through the speakers in only *one* room when you can fill the whole house with your sonic booms? Many companies now offer their own wireless multi-room sound systems that let you stick the iPod in a dock and broadcast its music through several remote speakers in other rooms.

For the products mentioned here, you don't even need an existing Wi-Fi network—great news if you're Wi-Fi-less or your network's already overloaded.

- **Eos Wireless.** For $250, you get an iPod base station that has its own set of speakers and one other remote speaker. You can scatter up to four additional wireless speakers in other rooms for about $130 a pop. If you want to better match the sound system to your home decor, you have a choice of black or white speakers. (*www.eoswireless.com*)

- **Creative Xdock Wireless.** You just need to plug the iPod into the Xdock and connect the X-Fi wireless receiver to the stereo or, say, a set of powered speakers upstairs. The basic system costs $200, but you can add on extra X-Fi receivers to other speakers in the house for $100 apiece, each with their own remote controls. (*www.creative.com*)

- **Sony S-Air Play.** This $400 package gets you a glossy iPod dock and two remote speaker units. Connect the dock, pictured here, to the stereo system (or use it solo). Snap the wireless cards into the remote speakers—

and the system is pretty much ready to rock. For big houses, up to 10 speakers can be used with the dock. Each satellite speaker unit also has an AM/FM tuner for real, live radio. The dock and speakers each have their own dedicated remote to control playback from every location. (*www.sonystyle.com*)

Connect the iPod to a Home Entertainment System

CD players that can play discs full of MP3 files cost less than $100. But if you have an iPod, you already have a state-of-the-art MP3 player that can connect to your existing stereo for under $20—or spend a little more and get the full iPod AV Club experience.

Connecting with an Audio Cable

To link the iPod to your stereo, you need the right kind of cable and a set of input jacks on the back of your receiver. Most audio systems come with at least one extra set of inputs (after accounting for the CD player, cassette deck, and other common components), so look for an empty AUX jack.

The cable you need is a Y-shaped cord with a 3.5 mm (1/8") stereo miniplug on one end and two bigger RCA plugs at the other end. The stereo miniplug is the standard connector for iPod-style headphones (and for speakers and microphones); RCA plugs are standard red-and-white tipped connectors for linking stereo components together.

You plug the smaller end into the iPod's headphone jack, and the RCA plugs into the left and right channel jacks on the back of your stereo. Most online iPod superstores like XtremeMac, Griffin Technology, DLO, and Belkin sell their version of the Y-shaped cable for iPod. There's a list of sites that sell helpful iPod stuff at the end of this chapter.

Adding an iPod Dock

Once you have your cables, you can also get an iPod dock to connect the player to your entertainment system. The benefit? Most docks come with remotes so you can control your iPod from the couch. The Universal Dock sells for $50 at *http://store.apple.com* and includes Apple's own miniature white remote control. The U-Dock comes with plastic adapters that serve as little iPod booster seats so the smaller-sized Nano can sit just as securely as a full-sized iPod.

In addition to linking iPod to stereo, the Universal Dock can also pipe video and photo slideshows from the iPod to your television set. For that movie magic to happen, though, you need to get an additional set of cables for the connection. Apple sells these, too—look, for example, for the Apple Composite AV Cable or the Apple Component AV Cable ($50 each) at *http://store.apple.com*.

Several companies make their own audio and video docks for iPods, but check to see which models each dock supports before you buy. Many video docks made for older iPods don't currently work with the Touch, Classic, or Nano.

Some newer models, like DLO's HomeDock HD, go the extra eye-candy mile by *upscaling*, or converting, the iPod's video content to HDTV-friendly resolutions. You can get resolutions of 720p or 1080i with an HDMI connection (common on high-end HDTV sets). With its included remote, the HomeDock HD, pictured below, lets you browse the iPod's content on the television screen. It sells for about $200 in electronics stores; details are at *www.dlo.com*.

Stream iTunes Music with Airport Express

What do you get when you mix an existing home Wi-Fi network with iTunes and Airport Express (Apple's portable wireless base station)? Music anywhere you want it. Stream your songs throughout your home by plugging one of these coaster-sized devices anywhere you've got a stereo. If you don't have an AirPort Express, you can buy one for $99 at *http://store.apple.com* and other places. Here's how to get started:

❶ **Plug the AirPort Express into an electrical outlet near the stereo (or a pair of powered speakers).** Repeat this step if there's anywhere else you want to beam your music.

❷ **Connect your stereo system or powered speakers to the AirPort Express.** After you plug the Airport Express into the wall, use a Y-shaped cable (the one with the two RCA plugs on one end and the miniplug on the other, mentioned earlier in this chapter) to connect the AirPort Express to the stereo system or a pair of powered speakers. If your system has a digital Toslink port, you can also use a digital fiber optic cable to connect the two instead for better sound. (Speakers that use a USB connection don't work with AirPort Express.)

❸ **Install the AirPort Utility software from the CD in the box.** The Utility program (Start→All Programs→Airport [Applications→Utilities→Airport]) walks you through the setup process, automatically picking up your Wi-Fi settings and prompting you to name the Airport Express. Naming it something like "Living Room Stereo" is helpful when it comes to using iTunes, as you'll see in the next step.

❹ **Open iTunes and look for a pop-up menu with the name of your AirPort Express.** Once you start up iTunes with the AirPort Express running, you'll notice a little pop-up menu at the bottom of the iTunes window (circled, facing page). If you've installed multiple Expresses, you'll see each listed in the pop-up menu.

❺ **Press Play.** With everything connected and turned on, select the base station in the iTunes pop-up menu and click the Play button to blast your playlists across your home. To play music simultaneously through more than one set of speakers, choose Multiple Speakers and then place a checkmark next to each speaker's name you wish to use.

Using the iPod Touch as a Remote

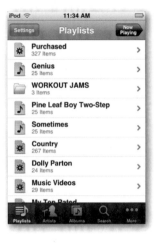

If you don't want to be tied to the computer to manage the tunes—and you have a Touch— there's a cool program called Remote in the iTunes App Store. Tapping into your Wi-Fi network, Remote lets you control your music from anywhere in the house. Even better, it's free.

Install the Remote app from the iTunes Store (Chapter 7) on your Touch. Tap the Remote icon and, on the next screen, tap Add Library. An icon for Remote appears in the iTunes Devices list. Click it and type in the four-digit code displayed on the Touch into the corresponding four boxes on the iTunes screen. Click OK and your iTunes library and playlists appear on the Touch screen. You can now play, pause, skip, and jump through your music library to your heart's content.

If you're having trouble geting Remote to show up in the iTunes window, open up Edit (iTunes)→Preferences→Devices and make sure there's a check in the box next to "Look for iPhone & iPod touch Remotes".

> **Note** If you don't have a Wi-Fi network but are ready to join the wireless revolution, you're in luck. The Airport Express also works as a full-fledged Wi-Fi router. Just follow the Airport Utility's setup instructions for creating a wireless network *and* for activating AirTunes (Apple's name for this whole streaming-music scenario).

Find a Power Source for the iPod

Your car's cigarette lighter can serve a far healthier role than its original purpose: It can breathe life into an iPod battery charger. You won't ever again have to worry about the iPod conking out in the middle of your favorite song when you're on the road. Several companies make these car chargers, including four well-known iPod accessory mavens:

- **PowerJolt SE.** This $20 doodad from Griffin Technology powers 'Pods on the road. It comes with a coiled cable to string between the PowerJolt and the iPod. It works with most modern dock-connecting iPods, including the Nano and the Touch; you can find it at *www.griffintechnology.com.*

- **DLO AutoCharger.** This stylish appliance powers your player and recharges it through the car's cigarette lighter, using three color-coded lights that let you keep tabs on your iPod's charging status. The $20 charger comes in either black or white and has a coiled cord that can stretch out to about five feet. You can get one at *www.dlo.com.*

- **Xtreme Mac InCharge Travel.** No matter if you move about by plane, train, or automobile, the InCharge Travel global charging kit keeps your iPod powered up. This $50 collection of cords and adapters includes a car charger, Empower adapter for commercial airline electrical systems, and regular electrical power adapter that you can use anywhere from an Amtrak train to a Japanese hotel room—plug adapters and voltage converters included. The company also sells a tubular $20 charger just to use in the car; all models are at *www.xtrememac.com.*

- **Belkin Auto Kit.** Designed for dock-connecting models, the Belkin Auto Kit includes a cable for charging your iPod from the car's cigarette lighter, plus an audio-out jack and adjustable amplifier that works with Belkin's TuneCast or cassette adapter (neither of which is included) for blasting iPod tunes through the car radio. The kit sells for $40 in the iPod accessories area at *www.belkin.com.*

Where to Find Cool iPod Stuff

Since the iPod's arrival in 2001, its accessories market has been growing by leaps and bounds. There are several online iPod superstores with a huge selection of merchandise, from stylish cases to snap-on FM radios. If you want to see what's out there without having to leave your desk, the bigger Podfocused Web shops include:

- **The Apple Store** (*http://store.apple.com*). Apple has pages and pages of products for all its iPod offspring. You can shop the store based on which model of iPod you have—which should help ease any compatability worries you have, as in "Hmmm, I wonder if this groovy speaker system will work with my fabulous new iPod Touch....?"

- **EverythingiCafe** (*store.everythingicafe.com*). Just about any iPod accessory you can think of can be found here—and some that haven't even crossed your mind until now.

- **Digital Lifestyle Outfitters** (*www.dlo.com/store*). One of the first makers of iPod accessories, DLO makes and sells a wide variety of cases, docks, car chargers, and even the iBoom box. The company also sells its own iPod Care Kit, a three-step cleaning solution to help clear up scratches and scuffs on beloved-but-battered iPods.

- **XtremeMac** (*www.xtrememac.com*). XtremeMac has an extremely large amount of iPod merchandise. It's notable for its SportWrap armband cases for active iPod lovers, creative charging solutions, alternative headphones, and compact home audio systems to boost your iPod's output throughout the house.

- **Griffin Technology** (*www.griffintechnology.com*). With its iTrip line of FM transmitters and its DirectDeck, Griffin's forte is products that get your iPod thumping through the car and home stereo speakers. The company also sells a handful of cases and items like the RadioShark, which is designed to add recordable broadcast radio to your computer and iPod.

Other companies like Belkin (*www.belkin.com*), Kensington (*www.kensington.com*), and Monster Cable (*www.monstercable.com*) have healthy iPod accessory sections on their sites, especially if you're looking for cables, docks, FM transmitters, and the like.

Computer and electronics stores like Fry's, Circuit City, and Best Buy usually have a section devoted to iPod cases and speakers. And as a sign of the iPod's mainstream cultural significance, even all-purpose suburban bazaars like Target also include a rack or two of iPod stuff for sale.

What to Do When the iPod Isn't Working Right

I t's bound to happen sometime: the iPod locks up, freaks out, or just isn't its usual cheerful self. Luckily, many iPod problems can be solved with a button-tap here, a battery charge there, and your portable Pod Life is back to normal.

Of course, the iPod is a little mini-computer in its own right, and there *are* bigger issues that are more involved or require the help of a technical expert. Figuring out what your iPod is trying to tell you when it's sick is the first step. This chapter explains what to do if your iPod's acting weird—and where to go if you need more information or can't fix it yourself.

Apple's Alphabet: The 5 (or 6) R's of iPod Repair

As posted in the growing iPod support section of its Web site (*www.apple.com/support/ipod/five_rs*) Apple recommends "The 5 Rs" whenever you encounter trouble with a Classic, Nano, or Shuffle. The Touch, unique among iPods, has its own six "Rs"—listed here at the bottom of the page.

Here's what each R stands for, along with a few more helpful details:

- **Reset** your iPod, as explained on the next page.

- **Retry** the connection by plugging the iPod into a different USB port on your computer.

- **Restart** your computer and check for any new software updates you may need to download and install.

- **Reinstall** your iPod and iTunes software with fresh versions downloaded from *www.apple.com/itunes*.

- **Restore** the iPod's software (also explained later in this chapter).

If you have an iPod Touch, the R's vary a bit and there's one more of them:

- **Recharge.** Make sure your Touch has gas in the battery tank.

- **Restart.** Press the Sleep/Wake button until the red Off/On slider appears. Slide the Touch off, then press Sleep/Wake to turn it on again.

- **Reset** your iPod Touch. The next page tells you how.

- **Remove.** Synced content may be sinking your Touch. Connect your iPod to iTunes and remove recently added stuff and resync.

- **Reset Settings.** Tap Settings→General→Reset→Reset All Settings. The option to erase all content and settings may also work, but it's drastic.

- **Restore.** Connect the Touch to iTunes and click Restore to reformat it.

The next few pages cover these steps and more, so you can avoid that last, painful R: *Ramming* your head into the wall when your iPod won't work.

Reset Your iPod

If your iPod Classic or Nano seems frozen, confused, or otherwise unrespon-sive, you can *reset* it without losing your music and data files. Some settings, like Bookmarks in long audio book files and On-The-Go Playlists may not be saved, but at least you can get things running again with this easy quick fix:

❶ Make sure the battery is charged and then slide the Hold switch on and off again.

❷ Press and hold down the Menu and center Select buttons.

❸ Hold both buttons down until you see the Apple logo appear on the screen. This could take up to 10 seconds to kick in, and you may have to do it twice, but keep pressing until you see the Apple logo.

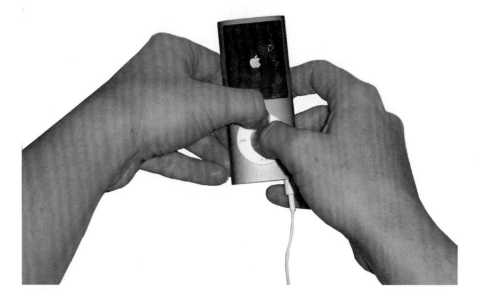

If the technology gods are smiling, the iPod goes through its little start-up sequence and then returns you to the main menu.

The reset procedure for the iPod Touch is easy to remember. Just hold down the two buttons that are *not* the volume rocker: the Sleep/Wake button on top and the Home button on the front. Let go when you see the Apple logo.

A stalled or befuddled iPod Shuffle may also need a good firm reset from time to time, but like the Shuffle itself, resetting it is a bit simpler than wrestling with other iPods: Turn the On/Off switch to the Off position, wait five seconds or so, and then flip it back to the On position.

Download and Reinstall iTunes and iTunes Updates

If iTunes is acting up, you may need to download and install a fresh version of the program. The latest version's always waiting at *www.apple.com/itunes/download*. The program itself may also alert you to a new version—or you can make sure it does in the future:

- If you use iTunes for Windows, choose Edit→Preferences→General and turn on "Check for updates automatically." If you prefer to check manually, choose Help→"Check for Updates".

- The Mac's Software Update program is designed to alert you, via a pop-up dialog box, about new updates for iTunes. If you've turned Software Update off (in System Preferences), however, you can run it manually by choosing Software Update from the Apple menu.

As with any software update, once you download the software, double-click the installer file's icon and follow along as the program takes you through several screens of upgrade excitement. If the version of iTunes you're installing is newer than the one you've got, you get Upgrade as a button option when you run the installer—and it usually takes less time to do the job.

If you're reinstalling the same version of the program, the iTunes installer may politely ask if you want to either *Repair* or even *Remove* the software. Choosing Repair can often fix damaged files or data iTunes needs to run properly. It can also be a quicker fix than fully removing the program and reinstalling it all over again.

Use the Diagnostics Tools in iTunes for Windows

With different PC hardware manufacturers out there and multiple versions of Windows in the mix, the PC side of the iTunes/iPod fence can be a little unpredictable. To help sort things out, iTunes 8 for Windows includes a feature called Diagnostics, which can help troubleshoot four categories of woes. Your choices include:

- **Network Connectivity.** These tests check your computer's Internet connection and its ability to access the iTunes Store.

- **DVD/CD Drive.** If you're having trouble getting music to import into iTunes from a CD—or can't burn your own discs, these tests inspect your PC's disc drive for problems and incompatibilities.

- **iPhone/iPod Connectivity.** These diagnostics don't actually test the iPod's own hardware or software, but they do examine the way your PC connects to your iPod.

- **iPhone/iPod Touch Sync.** These tests actually do test the iPod Touch's hardware and software to make sure it can transport the data you've chosen to sync.

To run the battery of tests, choose Help→Run Diagnostics, select a category, and then follow along onscreen. Each diagnostic program runs some tests and gives you a red, yellow, or green light. Click the Help button next to a red or yellow light to get troubleshooting help from Apple's Web site. (Green means groovy.) At the end, you can copy the results to the clipboard or save them to a text file for sharing with techies.

Update the iPod's Software

Updating the iPod's own internal software—which Apple does occasionally to fix bugs and add features—is much easier than it used to be, thanks to iTunes. No matter which model you have, iTunes 8 and later handles all iPod software updating chores.

If your iPod Nano or Classic is formatted for Windows, update it on a Windows PC; likewise, update a Mac-formatted iPod on a Macintosh. You can tell which system your iPod is formatted for by choosing, on the iPod, Settings→About. Press the Select button twice to get to the screen with the format info. (You need to update a Shuffle on the machine it's synced to to avoid erasing it.)

To make sure you have the latest version of the iPod's software, follow these steps:

❶ Connect your iPod to the computer and select it in the Source list.

❷ On the Summary tab, click the "Check for Update" button in the Version area. If your iPod is up to date, iTunes tells you so.

❸ If iTunes finds new iPod software, you'll be prompted to download it. Click the Downloading icon in the Source pane to monitor your download's progress (shown below). Sometimes iTunes will have already downloaded the new iPod software. In that case, just click the Update button in the iTunes main window.

❹ Follow the instructions onscreen.

iPod Software Update

Important Information

**iPod nano (4th generation) Software
Version 1.0.2**

• Support for iPod nano (4th generation)

For feature descriptions and complete instructions, see the user
guide for your iPod at:
    <http://www.apple.com/support/manuals/ipod/>

For more information about iPod nano, go to:
    <http://www.apple.com/ipodnano/>

To troubleshoot your iPod, go to:
    <http://www.apple.com/support/ipod/five_rs/>

< Back   Next >   Cancel

Older iPod models may require the use of an AC adapter to finish the update,
but newer iPods mainly just sit there quietly with a progress bar and an Apple
logo onscreen. Once all that goes away, your iPod screen returns to normal
and iTunes displays a message box letting you know the update is complete.

iPod

Updating "NanoPod"...

If you're updating your iPod Shuffle, play close attention to the progress bar
on the iTunes screen and follow any instructions given. Since the Shuffle has
no screen, iTunes is the place to look to see when the update is done—usually
by returning the Shuffle's icon to the Source list when it's good to go.

Note The section of Apple's Web site devoted to iPod support has grown tremendously
since the first iPod was released in 2001. You can find troubleshooting guides,
tutorials, and more for each iPod model at *www.apple.com/support/ipod*. If it's an
out-of-warranty hardware problem, try a specialized iPod repair shop like *www.
iresq.com/ipod* or *http://www.techrestore.com/ipod*. And when it does come time to
upgrade or replace your 'Pod, you can learn about Apple's recycling policy at *www.
apple.com/environment/recycling*.

Start Over: Restoring Your iPod's Software

Just like the operating system that runs your computer, your iPod has its own software that controls everything it can do. *Restoring* the iPod software isn't the same thing as updating it. Restoring is a much more drastic procedure, like reformatting the hard drive on your Mac or PC. For one thing, *restoring the software erases everything on your iPod.*

So restore with caution, and do so only if you've tried all the other trouble-shooting measures covered in this chapter. If you've decided to take the plunge, first make sure you have the most recent version of iTunes (flip back a page for information on that), and then proceed as follows:

❶ Start iTunes, and connect the iPod to your computer with its cable.

❷ When the iPod appears in the iTunes Source list, click its icon to see the Summary information (in the main area of the iTunes window).

❸ In the Summary area, click the Restore button.

Note Now, just because you've sucked the life out of your iPod doesn't mean that all your songs, videos, and so on are gone from iTunes. That's the beauty of the iPod-iTunes partnership: By storing everything in iTunes, you can always re-load it onto the iPod, as described on the next page.

❹ If you have an iPod Touch, iTunes gives you the chance to back up your settings—like your preferences for contacts and calendar syncing and other personalized data on the iPod. This means much less work getting your Touch all re-personalized after you reinstall its firmware. If you want to wipe every trace of your existence from the Touch, skip the backup.

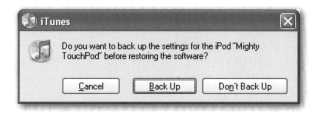

❺ Because restoring erases everything on your iPod, you get a warning message. If you're sure you want to continue, click Restore again.

❻ If you use a Mac, enter an administrator password; a progress bar appears on your iPod's screen. Leave the iPod connected to your computer to complete the restoration process. You may also see an Apple logo appear onscreen.

After the restore process is finished, the iTunes Setup Assistant window appears asking you to name your iPod and choose your syncing preferences—just like when you connected your iPod for the first time. Let the iPod automatically update or add your songs, photos, and videos back manually and see if this little procedure has fixed the iPod's ailment.

Tip If you manually manage your music and you restore the iPod's software, you'll lose any songs that are not already stored in your iTunes library. (For example, say you pulled some songs off another computer that you no longer have access to.) In that case you may want to get yourself a program that lets you harvest your songs off the iPod (*www.ilounge.com* lists several and Chapter 5 has suggestions).

Understanding the iPod's Battery Messages

Remember how you were taught that certain kinds of batteries (in laptops and camcorders, say) worked better if you occasionally fully drained and then recharged them? Forget it. You want to keep the iPod's lithium-ion battery charged *always*, or else you'll lose your clock, date, and other settings.

The color screen on the iPod Classic, Nano, and Touch shows a green battery that depletes as you use the player. When the battery icon turns red, it's time to recharge because you have less than 20 percent of your iPod's power left. The screenless Shuffle communicates its battery needs through a small colored light: green for a good charge, amber for partially drained, and red for a battery that needs juice pronto.

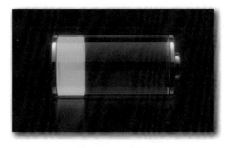 

Some iPods show a dull gray charging icon on the screen and won't turn on when the battery has run all the way down. This means the poor thing doesn't even have the energy to show its battery-charging color icon. On other models, you may see a yellow triangle icon next to a colorless battery graphic and the stern message, "Connect to Power".

Plug the iPod into the computer, or an optional AC adapter, and give it about half an hour of power to get back to its regular screen graphic. When the battery gets this depleted, you may also have to charge it up for a while to even get the iPod to show up in iTunes.

Note If you've had your iPod plugged in all night and the darn thing is still barely showing a charge, it's probably because something else went sleep besides you: the computer. An iPod won't charge properly when the computer goes into sleep, hibernation, or standby, so adjust your machine's power settings to make sure it doesn't conk out before the iPod gets juiced. An AC adapter, available at most iPod accessory shops (Chapter 12) lets you skip the whole computer-charging thing.

Apple's Tips for Longer iPod Battery Life

Apple has posted various recommendations on its Web site for how to treat the iPod battery to ensure a long life:

- Don't expose the iPod to extreme hot or cold temperature ranges. (In other words, don't leave it in a hot, parked car, and don't expect it to operate on Mt. Everest.)

- Use the iPod regularly (not that you wouldn't). And be sure to charge it at least once a month to keep that battery chemistry peppy.

- Put the iPod to sleep to conserve battery power. (Press the Play/Pause button until the iPod display goes blank and the iPod settles into slumber; on the Touch, click the Sleep/Wake button on top.)

- Take the iPod out of any heat-trapping cases before you charge it up.

- Use the Hold switch when you're not actively fiddling with the iPod's controls. This keeps it from getting bumped on automatically.

- When you see the Low Battery icon or message, plug the iPod into the computer or an electrical outlet with the AC adapter. The iPod battery indicator shows roughly how much charge is left in the battery.

- Features like the backlight and the equalizer—or jumping around your library—can make the battery drain faster, as can using big uncompressed file formats like AIFF.

- That wireless chip inside the iPod Touch is sapping power even if you're not trawling the Web. Save energy by turning it off when you don't need it at Settings→Wi-Fi.

Replace Your iPod's Battery

The iPod uses a rechargeable lithium-ion battery. Unlike players that run on Duracells, you can't easily pop out the old battery and replace it when the iPod wears out after repeated charging and use cycles.

Which is not to say you *can't* replace the iPod's battery. It just takes a little more time and effort. If your battery is too pooped to power your 'Pod, here are some options:

- You get a full year warranty on your iPod battery (two years with the optional AppleCare protection plan). But Apple itself offers an out-of-warranty battery replacement service for $59 at *www.apple.com/support/ ipod/service/battery*.

- Laptops For Less (*www.ipodbattery.com*), offers do-it-yourself iPod battery replacement kits for less than $20.

- OtherWorld Computing sells high-capacity NewerTech iPod batteries for all models of iPods. The company has instructional videos on their Web site, but will also replace the battery for you if you send them your iPod (*http://eshop.macsales.com/shop/ipod*).

- PDASmart.com will replace your iPod's ailing battery for $50 (parts and labor included) at *www.pdasmart.com/ipodpartscenter.htm*. The company can also fix broken screens and hard drives.

AppleCare—What It Is and Whether You Need It

You probably have an insurance policy on your house and car, so why not get one for your iPod? That's the logic behind getting the AppleCare Protection Plan for your iPod. The price for this peace of mind? The plan for the iPod Classic and Touch sells for $59, while coverage for the Nano and Shuffle is priced at $39.

When you buy a brand new iPod, you automatically get free telephone support to fix one problem within your first 90 days of iPod ownership, plus a year-long warranty on the hardware. If the iPod starts acting weird or stops working altogether, Apple will fix it for free or send you a replacement 'Pod.

If you buy the AppleCare Protection Plan (available in many places where you buy iPods or at *www.apple.com/support/products/applecareipod.html*), you get:

- One full year of free telephone support from the date of your iPod purchase
- Two full years of hardware protection from the date of your iPod purchase

Your iPod's earphones, battery, and cables are all covered under the plan. If you need a repair or replacement, your iPod's covered. Paying an extra $39 or $59 to get the extended warranty may not appeal to everyone, but if you want a little peace of mind with your new iPod, it's a small price to pay.

Index

X

Y

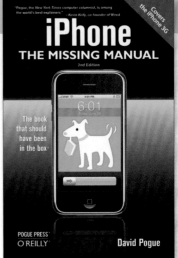
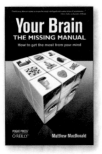

Try the online edition
free for 45 days

Keeping your competitive edge depends on having access to information and learning tools on the latest creative design, photography and web applications—but that's a lot easier said than done! How do you keep up in a way that works for you?

Safari offers a fully searchable library of highly acclaimed books and instructional videos on the applications you use every day. Best-selling authors offer thousands of how-to's, sharing what really works, and showing you how to avoid what doesn't. And with new content added as soon as it's published, you can be sure the information is the most current and relevant to the job at hand.

To try out Safari and the online edition of the *iPod: The Missing Manual*, Seventh Edition, FREE for 45 days, go to www.oreilly. com/go/safarienabled and enter the coupon code GMTJSAA

To see the complete Safari Library visit:
safari.oreilly.com